MEXICAN RECIPES

MEXICAN RECIPES

150 FIERY RECIPES SHOWN IN 250 VIBRANT PHOTOGRAPHS

JANE MILTON

southwater

This edition is published by Southwater
an imprint of Anness Publishing Ltd,
Blaby Road, Wigston, Leicestershire LE18 4SE;
info@anness.com

www.southwaterbooks.com;
www.annesspublishing.com

If you like the images in this book and would
like to investigate using them for publishing,
promotions or advertising, please visit our website
www.practicalpictures.com for more information.

Publisher: Joanna Lorenz
Recipes: Jane Milton
Photography: Simon Smith (recipes) and
  Janine Hosegood (reference)
Food styling: Caroline Barty (recipes) and
  Annabel Ford (reference)
Production Controller: Wendy Lawson

Designed and edited for Anness Publishing Ltd by
the Bridgewater Book Company Ltd

The publisher would also like to thank Corbis for
the use of the photograph on page 192 and South
American Pictures for the use of the photograph
on page 193.

A CIP catalogue record for this book is available
from the British Library.

Front cover shows Burritos with Chicken and Rice –
for recipe, see page 96.

PUBLISHER'S NOTE
Although the advice and information in this book
are believed to be accurate and true at the time of
going to press, neither the authors nor the publisher
can accept any legal responsibility or liability for any
errors or omissions that may have been made nor
for any inaccuracies nor for any loss, harm or injury
that comes about from following instructions or
advice in this book.

NOTES
Bracketed terms are intended for American
readers. For all recipes, quantities are given
in both metric and imperial measures and,
where appropriate, in standard cups and
spoons. Follow one set of measures, but
not a mixture, because they are not
interchangeable.

Standard spoon and cup measures are
level. 1 tsp = 5ml, 1 tbsp = 15ml, 1 cup =
250ml/8fl oz.

Australian standard tablespoons are 20ml.
Australian readers should use 3 tsp in place
of 1 tbsp for measuring small quantities.
American pints are 16fl oz/2 cups. American
readers should use 20fl oz/2.5 cups in place
of 1 pint when measuring liquids.

Electric oven temperatures in this book
are for conventional ovens. When using a fan
oven, the temperature will probably need to
be reduced by about 10–20°C/20–40°F.
Since ovens vary, you should check with your
manufacturer's instruction book for guidance.
The nutritional analysis given for each recipe
is calculated per portion (i.e. serving or item),
unless otherwise stated. If the recipe gives
a range, such as Serves 4–6, then the
nutritional analysis will be for the smaller
portion size, i.e. 6 servings. The analysis does
not include optional ingredients, such as salt
added to taste.
Medium (US large) eggs are used unless
otherwise stated.

Contents

Introduction

Mexican cuisine is as diverse and colourful as the country and different regions have developed their own specialities. Fish, meat, salsas and a huge variety of vegetables are the basis of Mexican cooking, fired up with chillies of every shape and size.

HISTORICAL INFLUENCES

In pre-Columbian Mexico there was already an established pattern of agriculture. Foods such as corn (maize), beans, chillies and peppers were widely cultivated, along with avocados, tomatoes, sweet potatoes, guavas, pineapples and vegetables, such as *jicama*, *chayote* and *sapote*.

When the Spaniards first arrived in Mexico in 1492, they tried and enjoyed local dishes made with corn, chillies, beans, tomatoes and chocolate. In turn, the Spanish had an influence on Mexican cooking. They brought livestock, such as pigs, which were warmly welcomed. Until this time, the native turkeys and the occasional wild boar were the only source of meat. Pigs also provided the local people with fat to cook with, a new concept for them.

In 1519 the Spanish adventurer Hernán Cortés landed near the site of present day Veracruz. Within three years he had conquered Mexico. Monks and nuns were sent from Spain to convert the local population to Catholicism and they also brought seeds, and soon citrus fruits, wheat, rice and onions augmented the supplies that served the Mexican kitchen and led to an even more diverse range of dishes.

The wider world still influences Mexican cuisine and its eating habits continue to evolve, adapt and embrace those from other cultures.

MEXICAN MEAL PATTERNS

Traditional meal patterns are still observed. The biggest meal of the day is eaten at lunchtime, sometimes followed by a siesta.

Desayuno is a light meal eaten first thing in the morning. It usually consists of a cup of coffee and a bread or pastry – perhaps *churros* or *pan dulce* (sweetened bread). Most Mexicans are then ready for something substantial by 11am. *Almuerzo* is similar to brunch, and usually includes an egg dish such as scrambled eggs with cheese. Coffee, milk or fruit juice washes everything down.

BELOW: *Mexican hot chocolate is made with hot milk and chocolate flavoured with almonds, cinnamon and vanilla.*

ABOVE: *Tacos are crisp tortilla shells that are eaten filled with salsa, beans and cheese.*

ABOVE: *This pecan cake is usually served with cream and redcurrants.*

ABOVE: *Queso de Chihuahua is a semi-soft cheese that is good for melting.*

Comida is the main meal of the day, generally eaten at a leisurely pace from about 3pm. The meal is made up of several courses. A light soup, such as *Tlalpeño,* a thin soup with chicken and avocado, is almost always served, and this is followed by a rice or pasta dish. The aptly named *platillo fuerte* – the phrase means "heavy dish" – is the main attraction and can be a meat or fish stew or a dish such as meatballs. This is accompanied by tortillas, salad and pot beans or refried beans. The clay pot used to cook the pot beans – *Frijoles de Olla* – adds flavour to them. Garlic, coriander, onion and stock with chillies are additional ingredients, and cream or cheese is stirred in just before serving. The meal closes with *postre* (dessert) and an after-dinner coffee.

Merienda is a light supper, this is often made up from the leftovers of the lunchtime *comida* dishes, which are wrapped in a tortilla to make a *burrito*. If a more substantial meal is required, a stew or *mole* might be served, with *Cafe con Leche* or hot chocolate to follow the food. *Merienda* is usually eaten between 8 and 9pm. When entertaining guests in the evening or on special occasions, *la cena* replaces the *merienda*, and is made up of two or three courses including dessert such as flan or a fruit platter, served any time between 8pm and midnight.

SNACK FOODS

Mexicans love to snack. Street food is very popular. In towns, stalls equipped with steamers sell *tamales* – little corn husk parcels filled with spiced meat or cheese – from first thing in the morning, so that shift workers can still have their *almuerzo* even if they cannot get home. Later in the day, the stalls sell corn soup or *menudo*, a soup made with tripe. Still more stalls are set up at lunchtime by women who serve home-made food to the workforce. In the evening, the stalls sell *quesadillas, enchiladas* and *antojitos* (little whims or nibbles). On the coast, traders sell prawns (shrimp) on skewers and *Ceviche* (marinated raw fish) threaded on sticks.

Salsas

Salsa simply means sauce, and Mexico is home to some of the finest. Hot and spicy, cool and refreshing, cooked or fresh, all are as versatile as they are varied. Their bright colours, incomparable flavours and adaptability make them indispensable to cooks, and their usefulness extends far beyond the boundaries of Mexican cuisine.

Guacamole

One of the best loved Mexican salsas, this blend of creamy avocado, tomatoes, chillies, coriander and lime now appears on tables the world over.

SERVES 6–8

4 medium tomatoes
4 ripe avocados, preferably fuerte
juice of 1 lime
1/2 small onion
2 garlic cloves
small bunch of fresh coriander (cilantro), chopped
3 fresh red fresno chillies
salt
tortilla chips, to serve

1 Cut a cross in the base of each tomato. Place the tomatoes in a heatproof bowl and pour over boiling water to cover. Leave the tomatoes in the water for 3 minutes, then lift them out using a slotted spoon and plunge them into a bowl of cold water. Drain. Remove the skins. Cut the tomatoes in half, remove the seeds, then chop the flesh roughly and set it aside.

2 Cut the avocados in half then remove the stones. Scoop the flesh out of the shells and place it in a food processor or blender. Process until almost smooth, then scrape into a bowl and stir in the lime juice.

3 Chop the onion finely, then crush the garlic. Add both to the avocado and mix well. Stir in the coriander. Remove the stalks from the chillies, slit them and scrape out the seeds with a small sharp knife. Chop the chillies finely and add them to the avocado mixture with the chopped tomatoes. Mix well.

4 Season to taste. Cover closely with clear film (plastic wrap) or a tight-fitting lid and chill for 1 hour before serving as a dip with tortilla chips. If it is well covered, guacamole will keep in the fridge for 2–3 days.

Nutritional information per portion: Energy 108kcal/445kJ; Protein 1.6g; Carbohydrate 3.1g, of which sugars 2.3g; Fat 9.9g, of which saturates 2.1g; Cholesterol 0mg; Calcium 13mg; Fibre 2.3g; Sodium 8mg.

Green tomatillo sauce

This sauce is a popular choice for pouring over enchiladas. Fresh tomatillos are difficult to obtain outside Mexico, but the sauce can be made with canned tomatillos.

SERVES 4 AS A SAUCE FOR A MAIN COURSE

2 fresh serrano chillies
4 garlic cloves, crushed
300g/11oz fresh tomatillos, husks
   removed and quartered, plus
   120ml/4fl oz/¹/₂ cup stock or water
   or 300g/11oz drained canned
   tomatillos, quartered, plus 60ml/
   4 tbsp/¹/₄ cup stock or water
15ml/1 tbsp vegetable oil
small bunch of fresh coriander (cilantro),
   chopped
120ml/4fl oz/¹/₂ cup double (heavy)
   cream (optional)
salt

1 Remove the stalks from the chillies, slit them and scrape out the seeds with a small knife. Chop the flesh roughly and place it in a food processor or blender with the garlic.

2 If using fresh tomatillos, place them in a pan and add the stock or water. Cook over a moderate heat for 8–10 minutes until the flesh is soft and transparent. Add the tomatillos to the processor with their cooking liquid and process for a few minutes until almost smooth.

3 If using canned tomatillos, put them in the food processor with the stock or water and the chillies and garlic. Process until almost smooth.

4 Heat the oil in a heavy-based pan and add the tomatillo purée. Reduce the heat and cook gently, stirring constantly, for about 5 minutes until the sauce thickens.

5 Add the coriander to the sauce, with salt to taste. Cook for a few minutes, stirring occasionally. Stir in the cream, if using, and warm the sauce through. Do not let it boil after adding the cream. Serve at once.

Nutritional information per portion: Energy 43kcal/179kJ; Protein 1.1g; Carbohydrate 2.9g, of which sugars 2.6g; Fat 3.1g, of which saturates 0.4g; Cholesterol 0mg; Calcium 10mg; Fibre 0.9g; Sodium 8mg.

Classic tomato salsa

This is the traditional tomato-based salsa that most people associate with Mexican food. There are innumerable recipes for it, but the basics of onion, tomato, chilli and coriander are common to every one of them. Serve this salsa as a condiment with a wide variety of dishes.

SERVES 6 AS AN ACCOMPANIMENT

3–6 fresh serrano chillies
1 large white onion
grated rind and juice of 2 limes, plus
    strips of lime rind, to garnish

8 ripe, firm tomatoes
large bunch of fresh coriander (cilantro)
1.5ml/¼ tsp caster (superfine) sugar
salt

1 Use three chillies for a salsa of medium heat; up to six if you like it hot. To peel the chillies, spear them on a long-handled metal skewer and roast them over the flame of a gas burner until the skins blister and darken. Do not let the flesh burn. Alternatively, dry fry them in a griddle pan until the skins are scorched. Place the roasted chillies in a strong plastic bag and tie the top of the bag to keep the steam in. Set aside for about 20 minutes.

2 Meanwhile, chop the onion finely and put it in a bowl with the lime rind and juice. The lime juice will soften the onion. Remove the chillies from the bag and peel off the skins. Cut off the stalks, then slit and scrape out the seeds with a sharp knife. Chop the flesh roughly and set aside.

3 Cut a small cross in the base of each tomato. Place the tomatoes in a heatproof bowl and pour over boiling water to cover. Leave the tomatoes in the water for 3 minutes, then lift them out using a slotted spoon and plunge into a bowl of cold water. Drain, then remove the skins completely.

4 Dice the peeled tomatoes and put them in a bowl. Add the chopped onion, which should have softened, together with the lime mixture. Chop the fresh coriander finely.

5 Add the coriander to the salsa, with the chillies and the sugar. Mix gently until the sugar has dissolved and all the ingredients are coated in lime juice. Cover and chill for 2–3 hours to allow the flavours to blend. Garnish with the strips of lime rind just before serving.

Nutritional information per portion: Energy 33kcal/138kJ; Protein 1.8g; Carbohydrate 5.3g, of which sugars 5g; Fat 0.6g, of which saturates 0.1g; Cholesterol 0mg; Calcium 34mg; Fibre 1.9g; Sodium 16mg.

Black bean salsa

This salsa has a very striking appearance. It is rare to find a black sauce and it provides a wonderful contrast to the more common reds and greens on the plate.

SERVES 4 AS AN ACCOMPANIMENT

130g/4½ oz/generous ½ cup black beans, soaked overnight in water to cover
1 pasado chilli
2 fresh red fresno chillies
1 red onion
grated rind and juice of 1 lime
30ml/2 tbsp Mexican beer (optional)
15ml/1 tbsp olive oil
small bunch of fresh coriander (cilantro), chopped
salt

1 Drain the beans and put them in a large pan. Pour in water to cover and place the lid on the pan. Bring to the boil, lower the heat slightly and simmer the beans for about 40 minutes or until tender. Drain, rinse under cold water, then drain again and leave until cold.

2 Soak the pasado chilli in hot water for about 10 minutes until softened. Drain, remove the stalk, then slit the chilli and scrape out the seeds with a small knife. Chop the flesh finely.

3 Spear the fresno chillies on a long-handled metal skewer and roast over the flame of a gas burner until the skins blister and darken. Do not let the flesh burn. Alternatively, dry fry in a griddle pan until the skins are scorched. Then place in a plastic bag and tie the top to keep the steam in. Set aside for 20 minutes.

4 Meanwhile, chop the red onion finely. Remove the chillies from the bag and peel off the skins. Slit them, remove the seeds and chop finely.

5 Tip the beans into a bowl and add the onion and both types of chilli. Stir in the lime rind and juice, beer, oil and coriander. Season with salt and mix well. Chill before serving.

Nutritional information per portion: Energy 109kcal/461kJ; Protein 6.6g; Carbohydrate 14g, of which sugars 1.1g; Fat 3.4g, of which saturates 0.5g; Cholesterol 0mg; Calcium 49mg; Fibre 2.7g; Sodium 9mg.

Pinto bean salsa

These beans have a pretty, speckled appearance. The smoky flavour of the chipotle chillies and the herby taste of the pasilla chilli contrast well with the tart tomatillos.

SERVES 4 AS AN ACCOMPANIMENT

130g/4¹/₂ oz/generous ¹/₂ cup pinto
   beans, soaked overnight in water
   to cover
2 chipotle chillies
1 pasilla chilli
2 garlic cloves, peeled
¹/₂ onion
200g/7oz fresh tomatillos
salt

1 Drain the beans and put them in a large pan. Pour in water to cover and place the lid on the pan.

2 Bring to the boil, lower the heat slightly and simmer the beans for 45–50 minutes or until tender. Drain, rinse under cold water, then drain again and tip into a bowl. Leave the beans until cold.

3 Soak the chipotle and pasilla chillies in hot water for about 10 minutes until softened. Drain, reserving the soaking water.

4 Remove the stalks, then slit each chilli and scrape out the seeds with a small sharp knife. Chop the flesh finely and mix it to a smooth paste with a little of the soaking water.

5 Roast the garlic in a dry frying pan over a moderate heat until the cloves start to turn golden. Crush them and add them to the beans.

6 Chop the onion and tomatillos and stir into the beans. Add the chilli paste and mix well. Add salt to taste, cover and chill before serving.

Nutritional information per portion: Energy 97kcal/410kJ; Protein 7g; Carbohydrate 16.8g, of which sugars 3.2g; Fat 0.7g, of which saturates 0.2g; Cholesterol 0mg; Calcium 32mg; Fibre 2.9g; Sodium 10mg.

Sweet potato salsa

Very colourful and delightfully sweet, this refreshingly tangy salsa makes the perfect accompaniment to hot, spicy Mexican dishes.

SERVES 4 AS AN ACCOMPANIMENT

675g/1¹/₂ lb sweet potatoes
juice of 1 small orange
5ml/1 tsp crushed dried jalapeño chillies
4 small spring onions (scallions)
juice of 1 small lime (optional)
salt

1 Peel the sweet potatoes and dice the flesh finely. Bring a pan of water to the boil. Add the sweet potato and cook for 8–10 minutes, until just soft. Drain off the water, cover the pan and put it back on the hob, having first turned off the heat. Leave the sweet potato for about 5 minutes to dry out, then tip into a bowl and set aside.

2 Mix the orange juice and crushed dried chillies in a bowl. Chop the spring onions finely and add them to the juice and chillies.

3 When the sweet potatoes are cool, add the orange juice mixture and toss carefully until all the pieces are coated. Cover the bowl and chill for at least 1 hour, then taste and season with salt. Stir in the lime juice if you prefer a fresher taste. The salsa will keep for 2–3 days in a covered bowl in the fridge.

Nutritional information per portion: Energy 155kcal/662kJ; Protein 2.3g; Carbohydrate 37.6g, of which sugars 11.1g; Fat 0.6g, of which saturates 0.2g; Cholesterol 0mg; Calcium 46mg; Fibre 4.3g; Sodium 70mg.

Chayote salsa

Chayote – or vegetable pear, as it is sometimes called – is a gourd-like fruit. It should be peeled before being eaten. The seed, which looks rather like a large, flat almond, is edible. The contrast between the crisp chayote, cool melon and hot habañero sauce makes this a spectacular salsa.

**SERVES 6 AS AN
ACCOMPANIMENT**

1 chayote, about 200g/7oz
¹/₂ small Galia or Cantaloupe melon
10ml/2 tsp habañero sauce or
    similar hot chilli sauce
juice of 1 lime
2.5ml/¹/₂ tsp salt
2.5ml/¹/₂ tsp sugar

1 Peel the *chayote*, then cut slices of flesh away from the stone. Cut the slices into thin strips. Cut the melon in half, scoop the seeds out, and cut each half into two pieces. Remove the skin and cut the flesh into small cubes. Place in a bowl with the *chayote* strips.

2 Mix the chilli sauce, lime juice, salt and sugar in a bowl or jug. Stir until all the sugar has dissolved. Pour over the melon and *chayote* mixture and mix thoroughly. Chill for at least 1 hour before serving. The salsa will keep for up to 3 days in the fridge.

Nutritional information per portion: Energy 16kcal/66kJ; Protein 0.4g; Carbohydrate 3.2g, of which sugars 2.9g; Fat 0.2g, of which saturates 0.1g; Cholesterol 0mg; Calcium 15mg; Fibre 0.5g; Sodium 16mg.

Jicama salsa

The jicama, *available in ethnic food stores, is a round, brown root vegetable with a texture somewhere between that of water chestnut and crisp apple. It can be eaten raw or cooked.*

SERVES 4 AS AN ACCOMPANIMENT

1 small red onion
juice of 2 limes
3 small oranges
1 *jicama*, about 450g/1lb
½ cucumber
1 fresh red fresno chilli

1 Cut the onion in half, then slice each half finely. Place in a bowl, add the lime juice and leave to soak.

2 Slice the top and bottom off each orange. Stand an orange on a board, then carefully slice off the peel and pith. Hold the orange over a bowl and cut between the membranes so that the segments fall into the bowl. Squeeze the pulp over the bowl to extract the remaining juice.

3 Peel the *jicama* and rinse it in cold water. Cut it into quarters, then slice finely. Add the *jicama* to the bowl of orange juice.

4 Cut the cucumber in half lengthways, then use a teaspoon to scoop out the seeds. Slice and add to the bowl. Remove the stalk from the chilli, slit it and scrape out the seeds with a sharp knife. Chop the flesh finely and add to the bowl.

5 Add the sliced onion to the bowl, with any remaining lime juice, and mix well. Cover and leave to stand for at least 1 hour before serving.

Nutritional information per portion: Energy 87kcal/371kJ; Protein 2g; Carbohydrate 20.5g, of which sugars 20.1g; Fat 0.3g, of which saturates 0g; Cholesterol 0mg; Calcium 64mg; Fibre 4g; Sodium 9mg.

Pumpkin seed sauce

The ancestors of modern-day Mexicans didn't believe in wasting food, as this traditional recipe proves. It is based upon pumpkin seeds, the flesh having been used for another dish.

**SERVES 4 AS AN
ACCOMPANIMENT**

130g/4½ oz raw pumpkin seeds
500g/1¼ lb tomatoes, quartered
2 garlic cloves, crushed
300ml/½ pint/1¼ cups chicken stock,
    preferably freshly made
15ml/1 tbsp vegetable oil
45ml/3 tbsp red chilli sauce
salt (optional)

1 Preheat the oven to 200°C/ 400°F/Gas 6. Heat a heavy frying pan until very hot. Add the pumpkin seeds and dry fry them, stirring constantly. The seeds will start to swell and pop, but they must not be allowed to scorch. When all the seeds have popped remove the pan from the heat.

2 Place the tomatoes on a baking tray. Roast in the hot oven for 45 minutes—1 hour, until charred and softened. Allow to cool slightly, then remove the skins using a sharp knife.

3 Put the pumpkin seeds in a food processor and process until smooth.

Add the tomatoes and process for a few minutes, then add the garlic and stock and process for 1 minute more.

4 Heat the oil in a frying pan. Add the red chilli sauce and cook, stirring constantly, for 2–3 minutes. Add the pumpkin seed mixture and bring to the boil, stirring all the time.

5 Simmer the sauce for 20 minutes, stirring frequently until the sauce has thickened and reduced by about half. Taste and add salt, if needed. If not serving immediately, the salsa will keep for up to a week in a covered bowl in the fridge.

Nutritional information per portion: Energy 201kcal/838kJ; Protein 6.1g; Carbohydrate 9.5g, of which sugars 4.8g; Fat 15.6g, of which saturates 1.8g; Cholesterol 1mg; Calcium 39mg; Fibre 2.9g; Sodium 50mg.

Nopales salsa

Nopales are the tender, fleshy leaves or "paddles" of an edible cactus known variously as the cactus pear and the prickly pear cactus. This grows wild in Mexico, but is also cultivated.

SERVES 4 AS AN ACCOMPANIMENT

2 fresh red fresno chillies
250g/9oz *nopales* (cactus paddles)
3 spring onions (scallions)
3 garlic cloves, peeled

1/2 red onion
100g/3 1/2 oz fresh tomatillos
2.5ml/1/2 tsp salt
150ml/1/4 pint/2/3 cup cider vinegar

1 Spear the chillies on a long-handled metal skewer and roast over the flame of a gas burner until the skins begin to blister and darken. Do not let the flesh burn. Alternatively, dry fry in a griddle pan until the skins are scorched. Place in a plastic bag and tie the top to keep the steam in. Set aside for 20 minutes.

2 Remove the chillies from the bag and peel off the skins. Cut off the stalks, then slit and scrape out the seeds. Chop the chillies roughly and set aside.

3 Remove the thorns from the *nopales*. Wearing gloves or holding each cactus paddle in turn with kitchen tongs, cut off the bumps that contain the thorns with a knife. Cut off and discard the thick base from each cactus paddle. Rinse the paddles well, cut into strips then cut the strips into small pieces.

4 Bring a large pan of lightly salted water to the boil. Add the cactus paddle strips, spring onions and garlic. Boil for 10–15 minutes, until the paddle strips are just tender. Drain, rinse under cold running water to remove any stickiness, then drain again. Discard the spring onions and garlic.

5 Chop the red onion and the tomatillos finely. Place in a bowl and add the cactus and chillies. Spoon the mixture into a large preserving jar, add the salt, pour in the vinegar and seal. Put the jar in the fridge for at least 1 day, turning the jar occasionally to ensure that the *nopales* are marinated. The salsa will keep in the fridge for up to 10 days.

Nutritional information per portion: Energy 18kcal/79kJ; Protein 1.5g; Carbohydrate 2.8g, of which sugars 2.4g; Fat 0.3g, of which saturates 0g; Cholesterol 0mg; Calcium 72mg; Fibre 1.5g; Sodium 6mg.

Roasted tomato salsa

Slow roasting these tomatoes to a semi-dried state results in a very rich, full-flavoured sweet sauce. The costeno amarillo chilli is mild and has a fresh light flavour, making it the perfect partner for the rich tomato taste. This salsa is great with tuna or sea bass.

SERVES 6 AS AN ACCOMPANIMENT

500g/1¼ lb tomatoes
8 small shallots
5 garlic cloves
sea salt
1 fresh rosemary sprig

2 costeno amarillo chillies
grated rind and juice of ½ small lemon
30ml/2 tbsp extra virgin olive oil
1.5ml/¼ tsp soft dark brown sugar

1 Preheat the oven to 160°C/325°F/Gas 3. Cut the tomatoes into quarters and place them in a roasting pan.

2 Peel the shallots and garlic and add them to the roasting tin. Sprinkle with sea salt. Roast in the oven for 1¼ hours or until the tomatoes are beginning to dry. Do not let them burn or blacken or they will have a bitter taste.

3 Leave the tomatoes to cool, then peel off the skins and chop the flesh finely. Place in a bowl.

4 Remove the outer layer of skin from any shallots that have toughened. Using a large, sharp knife, chop the shallots and garlic roughly, place them with the tomatoes in a bowl and mix.

5 Strip the rosemary leaves from the woody stem and chop them finely. Add half to the tomato and shallot mixture and mix lightly.

6 Soak the chillies in hot water for about 10 minutes until soft. Drain, remove the stalks, slit them and scrape out the seeds with a sharp knife. Chop the flesh finely and add it to the tomato mixture.

7 Stir in the lemon rind and juice, the olive oil and the sugar. Mix well, taste and add more salt if needed. Cover and chill for at least an hour before serving, sprinkled with the remaining rosemary. It will keep for up to a week in the fridge.

Nutritional information per portion: Energy 29kcal/123kJ; Protein 1.3g; Carbohydrate 5g, of which sugars 4.8g; Fat 0.5g, of which saturates 0.1g; Cholesterol 0mg; Calcium 32mg; Fibre 1.9g; Sodium 15mg.

Chilli strips with lime

This fresh relish is ideal for serving with stews, rice dishes or bean dishes. The oregano adds a sweet note and the absence of sugar or oil makes this a very healthy choice.

MAKES ABOUT 60ML/4 TBSP

10 fresh green chillies
1/2 white onion
4 limes
2.5ml/1/2 tsp dried oregano
salt

1 Roast the chillies in a griddle pan over a moderate heat until the skins are charred and blistered. Place the chillies in a strong plastic bag and tie the top to keep the steam in. Set aside for 20 minutes.

2 Meanwhile, slice the onion thinly and put it in a bowl. Squeeze the limes and add the juice to the bowl, with any pulp that gathers in the strainer. Stir in the oregano.

3 Remove the chillies from the bag and peel off the skins. Slit them, scrape out the seeds with a small sharp knife, then cut the chillies into long strips, which are called "rajas".

4 Add the chilli strips to the onion mixture and season. Cover and chill for at least 1 day before serving, to allow the flavours to blend. The salsa will keep for up to 2 weeks in a covered bowl in the fridge.

Nutritional information per portion: Energy 39kcal/165kJ; Protein 3g; Carbohydrate 5.9g, of which sugars 4.5g; Fat 0.6g, of which saturates 0g; Cholesterol 0mg; Calcium 40mg; Fibre 0.9g; Sodium 7mg.

Onion relish

This popular relish is typical of the Yucatán region and is often served with chicken, fish or turkey dishes. Try it with biscuits and cheese – it adds a spicy, tangy taste with no additional fat or sugar.

MAKES 1 SMALL JAR

2 fresh red fresno chillies
5ml/1 tsp allspice berries
2.5ml/¹⁄₂ tsp black peppercorns
5ml/1 tsp dried oregano
2 white onions
2 garlic cloves, peeled
100ml/3¹⁄₂fl oz/¹⁄₃ cup white wine vinegar
200ml/7fl oz/scant cup cider vinegar
salt

1 Spear the fresno chillies on a long-handled metal skewer and roast them over the flame of a gas burner until the skins blister. Do not let the flesh burn. Alternatively, dry fry the chillies in a griddle pan until the skins are scorched. Place the roasted chillies in a strong plastic bag and tie the top to keep the steam in. Set aside for 20 minutes.

2 Meanwhile, place the allspice, black peppercorns and oregano in a mortar or food processor. Grind slowly by hand with a pestle or process until coarsely ground.

3 Cut the onions in half and slice them thinly. Put them in a bowl. Dry roast the garlic in a heavy frying pan until golden, then crush and add to the onions in the bowl.

4 Remove the chillies from the bag and peel off the skins. Slit the chillies, scrape out the seeds with a small sharp knife, then chop them.

5 Add the spices to the onion mix, followed by the chillies. Stir in both vinegars. Add salt to taste and mix thoroughly. Cover the bowl and chill for at least 1 day before use.

Nutritional information per portion: Energy 218kcal/902kJ; Protein 8.3g; Carbohydrate 37.1g, of which sugars 24.2g; Fat 1.1g, of which saturates 0g; Cholesterol 0mg; Calcium 118mg; Fibre 6.6g; Sodium 25mg.

Guajillo chilli sauce

A tasty sauce that can be served over enchiladas or steamed vegetables.

SERVES 6 AS AN ACCOMPANIMENT

2 tomatoes, total weight about 200g/7oz, quartered
2 red (bell) peppers, cored, seeded and quartered
3 garlic cloves, in their skins
2 ancho chillies and 2 guajillo chillies
30ml/2 tbsp tomato purée (paste)
5ml/1 tsp dried oregano
5ml/1 tsp soft dark brown sugar
300ml/½ pint/1¼ cups chicken stock

1 Preheat the oven to 200°C/400°F/Gas 6. Place the tomatoes, peppers and garlic in a roasting pan and roast for 45 minutes, until slightly charred.

2 Put the peppers in a plastic bag and tie the top. Remove the skin from the tomatoes. Soak the chillies in boiling water for 15 minutes until soft.

3 Remove the peppers from the bag and rub off the skins. Halve and remove the cores and seeds, then chop the flesh and put it in a food processor or blender.

4 Drain the chillies, remove the stalks, then slit and scrape out the seeds. Chop and add to the peppers. Add the tomatoes. Squeeze the garlic, put in the blender with the other ingredients and process until smooth.

5 Pour the mixture into a pan, place over a moderate heat and bring to the boil. Lower the heat and simmer for 10–15 minutes until reduced to about half. Spoon into a bowl and serve hot or cold.

Nutritional information per portion: Energy 55kcal/230kJ; Protein 2.4g; Carbohydrate 10.4g, of which sugars 9.4g; Fat 0.6g, of which saturates 0.2g; Cholesterol 0mg; Calcium 19mg; Fibre 2.3g; Sodium 27mg.

Chipotle sauce

This sauce is ideal as an accompaniment or a marinade for barbecued food.

SERVES 6 AS AN ACCOMPANIMENT

500g/1¼ lb tomatoes, quartered
5 chipotle chillies
3 garlic cloves, roughly chopped
150ml/¼ pint/⅔ cup red wine
5ml/1 tsp dried oregano
60ml/4 tbsp clear honey
5ml/1 tsp American mustard
2.5ml/½ tsp ground black pepper and salt

1 Preheat the oven to 200°C/400°F/Gas 6. Place the tomatoes in a roasting pan. Roast for 45 minutes – 1 hour, until they are charred and softened.

2 Meanwhile, soak the chillies in a bowl of cold water for about 20 minutes until soft. Remove the stalks, slit the chillies and scrape out the seeds. Chop the flesh roughly.

3 Remove the tomatoes from the oven, let them cool slightly, then remove the skins. Chop the tomatoes and put them in a blender or food processor.

4 Add the chillies and garlic with the wine. Process until smooth, then add the oregano, honey, mustard and pepper. Process briefly, then taste and season with salt.

5 Scrape the mixture into a small pan. Place over a moderate heat and stir until the mixture boils. Lower the heat and simmer for about 10 minutes, stirring occasionally, until it has reduced and thickened. Spoon into a bowl and serve hot or cold.

Nutritional information per portion: Energy 76kcal/323kJ; Protein 1.1g; Carbohydrate 11.9g, of which sugars 11.9g; Fat 0.5g, of which saturates 0.1g; Cholesterol 0mg; Calcium 13mg; Fibre 1.3g; Sodium 40mg.

Adobo seasoning

Adobo means vinegar sauce, and this adobo is a chilli vinegar paste used for marinating pork chops or steaks. Adobos are widely used in the cooking of the Yucatán.

MAKES ENOUGH TO MARINATE 6 CHOPS OR STEAKS

1 small head of garlic
5 ancho chillies
2 pasilla chillies
15ml/1 tbsp dried oregano
5ml/1 tsp cumin seeds
6 cloves
5ml/1 tsp coriander seeds
10cm/4in piece of cinnamon stick
10ml/2 tsp salt
120ml/4fl oz/¹/₂ cup white wine vinegar

1 Preheat the oven to 180°C/350°F/Gas 4. Cut a thin slice off the top of the head of garlic, so that the inside of each clove is exposed. Wrap the head of garlic in foil. Roast for 45–60 minutes or until the garlic is soft.

2 Meanwhile, slit the chillies and scrape out the seeds. Put the chillies in a blender or a mortar. Add the oregano, cumin seeds, cloves, coriander seeds, cinnamon stick and salt. Process or grind with a pestle to a fine powder.

3 Remove the garlic from the oven. When it is cool enough to handle, squeeze the garlic pulp out of each clove and grind into the spice mix.

4 Add the wine vinegar to the spice and garlic mixture and process or grind until a smooth paste forms. Spoon into a bowl and leave to stand for 1 hour, to allow the flavours to blend. Spread over pork chops or steaks as a marinade, before grilling or barbecuing.

Nutritional information per portion: Energy 11kcal/45kJ; Protein 1g; Carbohydrate 1.5g, of which sugars 0.2g; Fat 0.1g, of which saturates 0g; Cholesterol 0mg; Calcium 6mg; Fibre 0.3g; Sodium 656mg.

Habañero salsa

This is a very fiery salsa with an intense heat level. A dab on the plate alongside a meat or fish dish adds a fresh, clean taste, but this is not for the faint-hearted.

SERVE SPARINGLY

5 dried roasted habañero chillies
4 dried costeno amarillo chillies
3 spring onions (scallions), finely chopped
juice of ¹/₂ large grapefruit or 1
    Seville orange
grated rind and juice of 1 lime
small bunch of fresh coriander (cilantro)
salt

1 Soak the habañero and costeno amarillo chillies in hot water for about 10 minutes until softened. Drain, reserving the soaking water.

2 Wear rubber gloves to handle the habañeros. Remove the stalks from all chillies, then slit them and scrape out the seeds with a small sharp knife. Chop the chillies roughly.

3 Put the chillies in a food processor and add a little of the soaking liquid. Purée to a fine paste. Do not lean over the processor – the fumes may burn your face. Remove the lid and scrape the mixture into a bowl.

4 Put the chopped spring onions in another bowl and add the fruit juice, with the lime rind and juice. Roughly chop the coriander.

5 Add the coriander to the chilli mixture and mix thoroughly. Add salt to taste. Cover and chill for at least 1 day before use. Serve the salsa sparingly.

Nutritional information: Energy 52kcal/218kJ; Protein 5.1g; Carbohydrate 5g, of which sugars 4.8g; Fat 1.4g, of which saturates 0g; Cholesterol 0mg; Calcium 145mg; Fibre 3g; Sodium 27mg.

Red rub

This "rub" or dry paste is frequently used in the Yucatán for seasoning meat.

MAKES ENOUGH FOR 1 JOINT OF MEAT OR 4 CHICKEN BREAST PORTIONS

10ml/2 tsp achiote (annatto) seeds
5ml/1 tsp black peppercorns
5ml/1 tsp allspice berries
5ml/1 tsp dried oregano
2.5ml/½ tsp ground cumin
5ml/1 tsp freshly squeezed lime juice
1 small Seville orange or ½ grapefruit

1 Put the achiote seeds in a mortar and grind them with a pestle to a fine powder. Alternatively, use a food processor. Add the peppercorns, grind again, then repeat the process with the allspice berries. Mix in the oregano and ground cumin.

2 Add the lime juice to the spice mixture. Squeeze the orange or grapefruit and add the juice to the mixture a teaspoonful at a time until a thick paste is produced.

3 Allow the paste to stand for at least 30 minutes so the spices absorb the juice and the paste is slightly dry and crumbly. When ready to use, rub the paste on to the surface of the meat, then leave to marinate for at least 1 hour before cooking, preferably overnight. The rub will keep for up to 1 week in a covered bowl in the fridge.

Nutritional information per portion: Energy 20kcal/82kJ; Protein 0.8g; Carbohydrate 2.5g, of which sugars 0.5g; Fat 0.8g, of which saturates 0g; Cholesterol 0mg; Calcium 49mg; Fibre 1.7g; Sodium 34mg.

Red salsa

Use this as a condiment with meat dishes, or as a dipping sauce for potato wedges.

MAKES ABOUT 250ML/8FL OZ/1 CUP

3 large tomatoes, quartered
15ml/1 tbsp olive oil
3 ancho chillies and 2 pasilla chillies
2 garlic cloves, peeled and left whole
2 spring onions (scallions)
10ml/2 tsp soft dark brown sugar
2.5ml/½ tsp paprika
juice of 1 lime
2.5ml/½ tsp dried oregano

1 Preheat the oven to 200°C/400°F/Gas 6. Place the tomatoes in a roasting pan. Drizzle over the oil. Roast for 40 minutes until slightly charred, then remove the skin.

2 Soak the chillies in hot water for 10 minutes. Drain, remove the stalks, slit and then scrape out the seeds. Chop finely. Dry roast the garlic in a pan until golden.

3 Slice one spring onion diagonally and set aside for the garnish. Chop the remaining spring onions and place in a bowl with the sugar, paprika, lime juice and oregano.

4 Put the tomatoes and chillies in a food processor or blender and add the garlic cloves. Process until smooth.

5 Add the sugar, paprika, lime juice, spring onions and oregano to the blender. Process briefly, then spoon into a pan and warm through before serving, or place in a bowl, cover and chill until required. Garnish with the spring onion.

Nutritional information per portion: Energy 158kcal/658kJ; Protein 2.1g; Carbohydrate 12.3g, of which sugars 12.3g; Fat 11.5g, of which saturates 1.6g; Cholesterol 0mg; Calcium 30mg; Fibre 0.6g; Sodium 8mg.

Soups and appetizers

As well as familiar, Western-style soups,

Mexico boasts "dry soups" in which

ingredients such as rice or corn tortilla

strips absorb excess liquid. This chapter

also features bocaditos, or "little bites",

an apt description for a range of dishes

that can be eaten as snacks or appetizers

or served together to make a quick meal.

Tortilla soup

There are several tortilla soups. This one is an aguada – or liquid – version, and is intended for serving as a starter or light meal. It is very easy and quick to prepare, or make it in advance and fry the tortilla mezes as it reheats. The crisp tortilla pieces add an unusual texture.

SERVES 4

4 corn tortillas, freshly made or a few
    days old
15ml/1 tbsp vegetable oil, plus extra
    for frying
1 small onion, finely chopped

2 garlic cloves, crushed
400g/14oz can plum tomatoes, drained
1 litre/1¾ pints/4 cups chicken stock
small bunch of fresh coriander (cilantro)
salt and ground black pepper

1 Using a sharp knife, cut each tortilla into four or five strips, each measuring about 2cm/¾in wide.

2 Pour vegetable oil to a depth of 2cm/¾in into a heavy pan. Heat the oil and add a small piece of tortilla. Fry until the tortilla floats on the top and bubbles at the edges.

3 Add a few tortilla strips to the hot oil and fry for a few minutes until crisp and golden brown, turning occasionally. Remove with a slotted spoon and drain on kitchen paper. Cook the remaining tortilla strips in the same way.

4 Heat the vegetable oil in a large pan. Add the onion and garlic and cook over a moderate heat for 2–3 minutes, stirring constantly with a wooden spatula, until the onion is soft and translucent. Do not let the garlic turn brown or it will give the soup a bitter taste.

5 Chop the tomatoes using a large sharp knife and add them to the onion mixture in the pan. Pour in the chicken stock and stir well. Bring to the boil, then lower the heat and allow to simmer for about 10 minutes, until the liquid has reduced slightly.

6 Chop the coriander. Add to the soup, reserving a little to use as a garnish. Season to taste.

7 Place a few of the crisp tortilla pieces in the bottom of four warmed soup bowls. Ladle the soup on top. Sprinkle each portion with the reserved chopped coriander and serve.

Nutritional information per portion: Energy 142kcal/595kJ; Protein 3.1g; Carbohydrate 19.6g, of which sugars 4.5g; Fat 6.2g, of which saturates 0.8g; Cholesterol 0mg; Calcium 63mg; Fibre 2.4g; Sodium 84mg.

Avocado soup

This delicious and very pretty soup is perfect for dinner parties and has a fresh, delicate flavour. You might want to add a dash more lime juice just before serving for added zest.

SERVES 4

2 large ripe avocados
300ml/¹/₂ pint/1¹/₄ cups crème fraîche
1 litre/1³/₄ pints/4 cups well-flavoured chicken stock
5ml/1 tsp salt
juice of ¹/₂ lime
small bunch of fresh coriander (cilantro)
2.5ml/¹/₂ tsp ground black pepper

1 Cut the avocados in half, remove the peel and lift out the stones. Chop the flesh coarsely and place it in a food processor with 45–60ml/3–4 tbsp of the crème fraîche. Process until smooth.

2 Heat the chicken stock in a pan. When it is hot, but still below simmering point, stir in the rest of the crème fraîche, with the salt.

3 Add the lime juice to the avocado mixture, process briefly to mix, then gradually stir the mixture into the hot stock. Heat gently but do not let the mixture approach boiling point.

4 Chop the coriander. Pour the soup into individual heated bowls and sprinkle each portion with coriander and black pepper. Serve immediately.

Nutritional information per portion: Energy 407kcal/1676kJ; Protein 3.3g; Carbohydrate 3.4g, of which sugars 2.1g; Fat 42.2g, of which saturates 21.7g; Cholesterol 78mg; Calcium 73mg; Fibre 3.2g; Sodium 24mg.

Chilled coconut soup

Refreshing, cooling and not too filling, this soup is the perfect antidote to hot weather. For a formal meal, it would be an excellent choice for serving after an appetizer, to refresh the palate.

SERVES 6

1.2 litres/2 pints/5 cups milk
225g/8oz/2²/₃ cups desiccated (dry unsweetened shredded) coconut
400ml/14fl oz/1²/₃ cups coconut milk
400ml/14fl oz/1²/₃ cups chicken stock
200ml/7fl oz/scant 1 cup double (heavy) cream
2.5ml/¹/₂ tsp salt
2.5ml/¹/₂ tsp ground white pepper
5ml/1 tsp caster (superfine) sugar
small bunch of fresh coriander (cilantro)

1 Pour the milk into a large pan. Bring to the boil, stir in the coconut, lower the heat and simmer for 30 minutes. Spoon into a food processor and process until smooth – pause often and scrape down the sides of the bowl.

2 Rinse the pan to remove any coconut that remains, pour in the processed mixture and add the coconut milk. Stir in the chicken stock, cream, salt, pepper and sugar. Bring the mixture to the boil, stirring occasionally, then lower the heat and cook for 10 minutes.

3 Reserve a few coriander leaves, then chop the rest finely and stir into the soup. Pour into a large bowl, let it cool, then cover and chill. Taste and adjust the seasoning. Garnish with coriander leaves, and serve in chilled bowls.

Nutritional information per portion: Energy 597kcal/2474kJ; Protein 10.8g; Carbohydrate 16.9g, of which sugars 16.9g; Fat 54.6g, of which saturates 40.8g; Cholesterol 69mg; Calcium 317mg; Fibre 6.7g; Sodium 188mg.

Corn soup

Quick and easy to prepare, this colourful soup has a sweet and creamy flavour.

SERVES 6

2 red (bell) peppers
30ml/2 tbsp vegetable oil
1 medium onion, finely chopped
500g/1¼ lb/3–4 cups corn niblets, thawed
    if frozen
750ml/1¼ pints/3 cups chicken stock
150ml/¼ pint/⅔ cup single (light) cream
salt and ground black pepper

1 Dry fry the peppers in a griddle pan over a moderate heat until the skins are blistered all over. Put in a plastic bag, set aside for 20 minutes, then remove and peel off the skins. Cut in half and scoop out the seeds and cores. Set one pepper aside. Cut the other into 1cm/½ in dice.

2 Heat the oil in a large pan. Add the onion and fry over a low heat for about 10 minutes, until translucent and soft. Stir in the diced pepper and corn and fry for 5 minutes over a moderate heat.

3 Spoon the contents of the pan into a food processor, pour in the stock and process until almost smooth.

4 Return the soup to the pan and reheat. Gently stir in the cream, with salt and pepper to taste. Core, seed and cut the reserved pepper into thin strips and add half of it to the pan. Serve the soup in heated bowls, garnished with the remaining pepper strips.

Nutritional information per portion: Energy 328kcal/1367kJ; Protein 7.6g; Carbohydrate 27.7g, of which sugars 10.4g; Fat 21.6g, of which saturates 12.8g; Cholesterol 45mg; Calcium 126mg; Fibre 1.5g; Sodium 463mg.

Tlalpeño-style soup

This simple chicken soup originates from Tlalpan, a suburb of Mexico City.

SERVES 6

1.5 litres/2½ pints/6¼ cups chicken stock
½ chipotle chilli, seeded
2 skinless chicken breast fillets
1 medium avocado
4 spring onions (scallions), finely sliced
400g/14oz can chickpeas, drained
salt and ground black pepper
75g/3oz/¾ cup grated Cheddar cheese, to serve

1 Pour the stock into a large pan and add the dried chilli. Bring to the boil, add the whole chicken fillets, then lower the heat and simmer for about 10 minutes or until the chicken is cooked. Remove the chicken from the pan and let it cool a little.

2 Using two forks, shred the chicken into small pieces. Set it aside. Pour the stock and chilli into a blender or food processor and process until smooth. Return the stock to the pan.

3 Cut the avocado in half, remove the skin and seed, then slice the flesh into 2cm/¾ in pieces. Add it to the stock, with the spring onions and chickpeas. Return the shredded chicken to the pan, with salt and pepper to taste, and heat gently.

4 Spoon the soup into heated bowls. Sprinkle grated cheese on top of each portion and serve immediately.

Nutritional information per portion: Energy 239kcal/1005kJ; Protein 24.8g; Carbohydrate 11.3g, of which sugars 0.6g; Fat 10.6g, of which saturates 4.2g; Cholesterol 60mg; Calcium 141mg; Fibre 3.4g; Sodium 291mg.

Empanadas with ropas viejas

The filling for these empanadas is traditionally made with meat that is cooked until it is so tender that it can be torn apart with forks. It resembles tattered cloth, which is how it came to be known as ropa vieja, *which means "old clothes".*

SERVES 6 (12 EMPANADAS)

150g/5oz/1 cup *masa harina*
30ml/2 tbsp plain (all-purpose) flour
2.5ml/¹/₂ tsp salt
120–150ml/4–5fl oz/¹/₂–²/₃ cup
    warm water
15ml/1 tbsp oil, plus extra for frying
250g/9oz lean minced pork

1 garlic clove, crushed
3 tomatoes
2 ancho chillies, deseeded and
    finely chopped
¹/₂ small onion, finely chopped
2.5ml/¹/₂ tsp ground cumin
2.5ml/¹/₂ tsp salt

1 Mix the *masa harina*, flour and salt in a bowl. Add enough water to make a smooth, but not sticky, dough. Knead briefly, wrap in clear film (plastic wrap) and set aside.

2 Heat 15ml/1 tbsp oil in a pan. Add the pork and cook, stirring frequently, until it has browned evenly. Stir in the garlic and cook for 2 minutes more. Remove from the heat and set the pan aside.

3 Remove the skins from the tomatoes. Chop the flesh and put in a bowl. Add the chillies, onion and cumin. Stir into the pan containing the pork. Cook over a moderate heat for 10 minutes, stirring occasionally. Season with salt.

4 To make the tortillas, divide the dough into 12 pieces and roll each piece into a ball. Open a tortilla press and line both sides with plastic. Put a ball of dough on the press and flatten it into a 7.5cm/3in round. Use the remaining dough balls to make more tortillas in the same way.

5 Spoon a little of the meat mixture on one half of each tortilla, working quickly to stop the dough from drying out. Dampen the edges of the dough with a little water and fold, then seal the edges.

6 Heat a little oil in a large frying pan. Fry the empanadas in batches until crisp and golden on both sides, turning at least once. Serve hot or cold.

Nutritional information per portion: Energy 228kcal/951kJ; Protein 10.4g; Carbohydrate 24.5g, of which sugars 2.2g; Fat 9.7g, of which saturates 1.4g; Cholesterol 21mg; Calcium 16mg; Fibre 1.4g; Sodium 28mg.

Panuchos

These stuffed tortillas are a bit fiddly to make, but well worth the effort. This dish is particularly popular in the Yucatán.

SERVES 6 (12 PANUCHOS)

150g/5oz/1 cup *masa harina*
pinch of salt
120ml/4fl oz/½ cup warm water
2 skinless chicken breast fillets
5ml/1 tsp dried oregano
150g/5oz/about 1 cup *Frijoles de Olla*,
    blended to a smooth purée (paste)
2 hard-boiled eggs, sliced
oil, for shallow frying
salt and ground black pepper
Onion Relish, to serve

1 Mix the *masa harina* and salt in a bowl. Add the warm water to make a dough. Knead until smooth, wrap in clear film (plastic wrap) and leave for 1 hour.

2 Put the chicken in a pan, add the oregano and cover with water. Bring to the boil, reduce the heat and simmer for until cooked. Remove the chicken, let cool and shred.

3 Roll the dough into 12 balls. Open a tortilla press and line both sides with plastic. Flatten each dough ball into a 6cm/2½in round in the press.

4 Cook each tortilla in a hot frying pan for 15–20 seconds on each side. After a further 15 seconds on one side remove and wrap in a towel.

5 Cut a slit in each tortilla, about 1cm/½in deep around the rim. Put a spoonful of the bean purée and a slice of hard-boiled egg in each slit.

6 Heat the oil in a large frying pan. Fry the tortilla pockets until crisp and golden brown. Drain on kitchen paper, place on individual serving plates and top with chicken and relish. Season to taste and serve.

Nutritional information per portion: Energy 258kcal/1080kJ; Protein 19.4g; Carbohydrate 24.9g, of which sugars 0.4g; Fat 9g, of which saturates 1.4g; Cholesterol 98mg; Calcium 20mg; Fibre 1.7g; Sodium 55mg.

Sopes with **picadillo**

These are small, thick tortillas made with masa harina *with crimped edges, which are filled like tarts. The filling –* picadillo *– is very popular in Mexico and is used in many different recipes.*

SERVES 6

250g/9oz/scant 2 cups *masa harina*
2.5ml/¹/₂ tsp salt
50g/2oz/¹/₄ cup chilled lard, grated
300ml/¹/₂ pint/1¹/₄ cups warm water
15ml/1 tbsp vegetable oil
250g/9oz lean minced (ground) beef
2 garlic cloves, crushed
1 red (bell) pepper, seeded and chopped
60ml/4 tbsp dry sherry
15ml/1 tbsp tomato purée (paste)
2.5ml/¹/₂ tsp ground cumin
5ml/1 tsp ground cinnamon
1.5ml/¹/₄ tsp ground cloves
2.5ml/¹/₂ tsp ground black pepper
25g/1oz/3 tbsp raisins
25g/1oz/¹/₄ cup flaked (sliced) almonds
fresh parsley sprigs, to garnish

1 Put the *masa harina* and salt in a large bowl. Rub in the lard. Add the water, a little at a time, to make a dough. Knead on a lightly floured surface until smooth. Set aside.

2 Heat the oil in a pan. Add the beef and cook over a high heat, stirring until it has browned. Stir in the garlic and continue cooking for 2–3 minutes, stirring occasionally.

3 Stir in the red pepper, sherry, tomato purée and spices. Cook for 5 minutes more, then add the raisins

and almonds. Lower the heat and simmer for 10 minutes. Keep hot.

4 Divide the dough into six balls. Open a tortilla press and line both sides with plastic. Flatten each ball into a 10cm/4in round.

5 Heat a griddle or frying pan until hot. Add a round and fry briefly on both sides until the underside begins to brown and blister. Slide on to a plate and crimp the rim. Fill with the beef and keep hot while making the others. Garnish with parsley.

Nutritional information per portion: Energy 441kcal/1840kJ; Protein 15.9g; Carbohydrate 45.3g, of which sugars 8.5g; Fat 10.3g, of which saturates 2.1g; Cholesterol 24mg; Calcium 28mg; Fibre 2.1g; Sodium 42mg.

Taquitos with beef

Miniature soft corn tortillas moulded around a tasty filling and served warm. Unless you have access to miniature fresh corn tortillas, you will need a tortilla press.

SERVES 12

500g/1¼ lb rump (round) steak, diced
    into 1cm/½ in pieces
2 garlic cloves, peeled and left whole
750ml/1¼ pints/3 cups beef stock
150g/5oz/1 cup *masa harina*
pinch of salt
120ml/4fl oz/½ cup warm water
7.5ml/1½ tsp dried oregano
2.5ml/½ tsp ground cumin
30ml/2 tbsp tomato purée (paste)
2.5ml/½ tsp caster (superfine) sugar
salt and ground black pepper
shredded lettuce and Onion Relish,
    to serve

1 Put the beef and garlic in a pan and cover with the stock. Bring to the boil, lower the heat and simmer for 10–15 minutes, until the meat is tender. Transfer the meat to a clean pan and set it aside. Reserve the stock.

2 Mix the *masa harina* and salt in a bowl. Add the water, a little at a time, to make a dough. Knead this dough on a floured surface for 4 minutes until smooth. Wrap in clear film (plastic wrap) and leave to rest for 1 hour.

3 Divide the dough into 12 small balls. Open a tortilla press and line both sides with plastic. Put a ball on the press and bring the top down to flatten it into a 5–6cm/2–2½ in round. Repeat with the remaining dough balls.

4 Heat a griddle or frying pan until hot. Cook each tortilla for 15–20 seconds on each side, and then for a further 15 seconds on the first side. Keep the tortillas warm and soft by folding them inside a slightly damp dishtowel.

5 Add the oregano, cumin, tomato purée and sugar to the pan containing the beef, with 2 tablespoons of the reserved stock. Cook gently for a few minutes. Place a little lettuce, filling and relish on each tortilla and serve.

Nutritional information per portion: Energy 109kcal/458kJ; Protein 11.8g; Carbohydrate 10g, of which sugars 0.7g; Fat 2.4g, of which saturates 0.8g; Cholesterol 28mg; Calcium 4mg; Fibre 0.4g; Sodium 36mg.

Quesadillas

These cheese-filled tortillas are the Mexican equivalent of toasted sandwiches. Serve them as soon as they are cooked, or they will become chewy.

SERVES 4

200g/7oz mozzarella, Monterey Jack or
    mild Cheddar cheese
1 fresh fresno chilli (optional)
8 wheat flour tortillas, about 15cm/6in
    across
Onion Relish or Classic Tomato Salsa,
    to serve

1 If using mozzarella cheese, it must be drained thoroughly and then patted dry and sliced into thin strips. Monterey Jack and Cheddar cheese should both be coarsely grated. Set the cheese aside in a bowl.

2 If using the chilli, dry fry it in a griddle pan until the skin is scorched. Place the roasted chilli in a strong plastic bag and tie the top to keep the steam in. Set aside for 20 minutes.

3 Remove the chilli from the bag and peel off the skin. Cut off the stalk, then slit the chilli and scrape out the seeds. Cut the flesh into eight thin strips.

4 Warm a large frying pan or griddle. Place one tortilla on the pan or griddle at a time, sprinkle about an eighth of the cheese on to one half and add a strip of chilli, if using. Fold the tortilla over the cheese and press the edges together gently to seal. Cook the filled tortilla for 1 minute, then turn over and cook the other side for 1 minute.

5 Remove the filled tortilla from the pan or griddle, cut it into three triangles or four strips and serve at once, with the onion relish or tomato salsa.

Nutritional information per portion: Energy 372kcal/1559kJ; Protein 17.2g; Carbohydrate 37.4g, of which sugars 0.8g; Fat 17g, of which saturates 10.9g; Cholesterol 49mg; Calcium 438mg; Fibre 1.5g; Sodium 537mg.

Tortas

The essential ingredients of a torta are refried beans and chillies, everything else is subject to change and personal taste. Traditionally they are made using rolls called **teleras.**

SERVES 2

2 fresh jalapeño chillies
juice of 1/2 lime
2 French bread rolls or 2 pieces of
    French bread
115g/4oz/2/3 cup refried beans
150g/5oz roast pork
2 small tomatoes, sliced
115g/4oz Cheddar cheese, sliced
small bunch of fresh coriander (cilantro)
30ml/2 tbsp crème fraîche

1 Cut the chillies in half, scrape out the seeds, then cut the flesh into thin strips. Put it in a bowl, pour over the lime juice and leave to stand.

2 If using rolls, slice them in half and remove some of the crumb so that they are slightly hollowed. If using French bread, slice each piece in half lengthways. Set the top of each piece of bread or roll aside and spread the bottom halves with the refried beans.

3 Cut the pork into thin shreds and put these on top of the refried beans. Top with the tomato slices. Drain the jalapeño strips and put them on top of the tomato slices. Add the cheese and sprinkle with coriander leaves.

4 Turn the top halves of the bread or rolls over, so that the cut sides are uppermost, and spread these with crème fraîche. Sandwich back together again and serve.

Nutritional information per portion: Energy 703kcal/2956kJ; Protein 42.9g; Carbohydrate 72.4g, of which sugars 8.4g; Fat 27.8g, of which saturates 16.4g; Cholesterol 108mg; Calcium 570mg; Fibre 7.8g; Sodium 1329mg.

Mexican rice

Versions of this dish – a relative of Spanish rice – are popular all over South America. Classified as a sopa seca or dry soup, it is a delicious medley of rice, tomatoes and aromatic flavourings.

SERVES 6

200g/7oz/1 cup long grain rice
200g/7oz can chopped tomatoes in
    tomato juice
1/2 onion, roughly chopped
2 garlic cloves, roughly chopped
30ml/2 tbsp vegetable oil
450ml/3/4 pint/scant 2 cups chicken
    stock
2.5ml/1/2 tsp salt
3 fresh fresno chillies or other fresh
    green chillies, trimmed
150g/5oz/1 cup frozen peas (optional)
ground black pepper

1 Put the rice in a heatproof bowl and pour over boiling water to cover. Stir once, then leave to stand for 10 minutes. Tip into a strainer, rinse under cold water, then drain again. Set aside to dry slightly.

2 Meanwhile, pour the tomatoes and juice into a food processor or blender, add the onion and garlic and process until smooth.

3 Heat the oil in a large, heavy pan, add the rice and cook over a moderate heat until it becomes golden brown. Stir occasionally.

4 Add the tomato mixture and stir until all the liquid has been absorbed. Stir in the stock, salt, whole chillies and peas, if using. Continue to cook the mixture, stirring occasionally, until all the liquid has been absorbed and the rice is just tender.

5 Remove the pan from the heat, cover it with a tight-fitting lid and leave it to stand in a warm place for 5–10 minutes. Remove the chillies, fluff up the rice lightly and serve, sprinkled with black pepper. The chillies may be used as a garnish, if liked.

Nutritional information per portion: Energy 164kcal/685kJ; Protein 3g; Carbohydrate 28.6g, of which sugars 1.8g; Fat 4g, of which saturates 0.5g; Cholesterol 0mg; Calcium 25mg; Fibre 0.8g; Sodium 6mg.

Chillies rellenos

Stuffed chillies are popular all over Mexico. The type of chilli used differs from region to region, but larger chillies are obviously easier to stuff than smaller ones.

MAKES 6

6 fresh poblano or Anaheim chillies
2 potatoes, total weight about
    400g/14oz
200g/7oz/scant 1 cup cream cheese
200g/7oz/1³⁄₄ cups grated mature
    (sharp) Cheddar cheese
5ml/1 tsp salt

2.5ml/¹⁄₂ tsp ground black pepper
2 eggs, separated
115g/4oz/1 cup plain (all-purpose) flour
2.5ml/¹⁄₂ tsp white pepper
oil, for frying
chilli flakes, to garnish (optional)

1 Make a slit down one side of each chilli. Place in a dry frying pan over a moderate heat, turning frequently until the skins blister. Place in a plastic bag and set aside for 20 minutes. Peel off the skins and remove the seeds through the slits. Dry with kitchen paper and set aside.

2 Scrub or peel the potatoes and cut into 1cm/¹⁄₂ in dice. Bring a large pan of water to the boil, add the potatoes and simmer for 5 minutes or until the potatoes are just tender. Do not overcook. Drain them thoroughly.

3 Put the cream cheese in a bowl and stir in the grated cheese, with 2.5ml/¹⁄₂ tsp of the salt and the black pepper. Add the potato and mix gently. Spoon some of the potato filling into each chilli. Put on a plate, cover with clear film (plastic wrap) and chill for 1 hour.

4 Put the egg whites in a clean, grease-free bowl and whisk them to firm peaks. In a separate bowl, beat the yolks until pale, then fold in the whites. Scrape the mixture on to a shallow dish. Spread out the flour in another shallow dish and season it with the remaining salt and the white pepper.

5 Heat the oil for deep frying to 190°C/375°F. Coat a few chillies first in flour and then in egg before adding carefully to the hot oil. Fry the chillies in batches until golden and crisp. Drain on kitchen paper and serve hot, garnished with a sprinkle of chilli flakes for extra heat, if desired.

Nutritional information per portion: Energy 605kcal/2512kJ; Protein 18.5g; Carbohydrate 30.8g, of which sugars 1.9g; Fat 45.4g, of which saturates 27.7g; Cholesterol 159mg; Calcium 385mg; Fibre 1.5g; Sodium 478mg.

Spiced plantain chips

Plantains are more starchy than the bananas to which they are related, and must be cooked before being eaten. In Latin America the fruit is used much as a potato would be. This snack has a lovely sweet taste, which is balanced by the heat from the chilli powder and sauce.

SERVES 4 AS AN APPETIZER OR SNACK

2 large plantains
oil, for shallow frying
2.5ml/¹/₂ tsp chilli powder
5ml/1 tsp ground cinnamon
hot chilli sauce, to serve

1 Peel the plaintains. Cut off and throw away the ends, then slice the fruit into rounds, cutting slightly on the diagonal to give larger, flatter slices.

2 Pour the oil for frying into a small frying pan, to a depth of about 1cm/ ¹/₂ in. Heat the oil until it is very hot, watching it closely all the time. Test by carefully adding a slice of plantain; it should float and the oil should immediately bubble up around it.

3 Fry the plantain slices in small batches or the temperature of the oil will drop. When they are golden brown remove from the oil with a slotted spoon and drain on kitchen paper.

4 Mix the chilli powder with the cinnamon. Put the plantain chips on a serving plate, sprinkle them with the chilli and cinnamon mixture and serve immediately, with a small bowl of hot chilli sauce for dipping.

Nutritional information per portion: Energy 193kcal/806kJ; Protein 1.1g; Carbohydrate 22.7g, of which sugars 4.3g; Fat 11.5g, of which saturates 1.4g; Cholesterol 0mg; Calcium 23mg; Fibre 1.6g; Sodium 14mg.

Popcorn with lime and chilli

The popcorn that comes in a carton at the cinema doesn't come close to this Mexican speciality. The lime juice and chilli powder are inspired additions, and it is suitable to serve with drinks.

MAKES 1 LARGE BOWL

30ml/2 tbsp vegetable oil
225g/8oz/1¼ cups corn kernels for
    popcorn
10ml/2 tsp chilli powder
juice of 2 limes

1 Heat the oil in a large, heavy frying pan until it is very hot. Add the popcorn and immediately cover the pan with a lid and reduce the heat.

2 After a few minutes the corn should start to pop. Resist the temptation to lift the lid to check. Shake the pan occasionally so that all corn will be cooked and browned.

3 When the sound of popping corn has stopped, quickly remove the pan from the heat and allow to cool slightly. Take off the lid and with a spoon lift out and discard any kernels that have not popped as they are inedible.

4 Add the chilli powder. Shake the pan again and again to make sure that all of the corn is covered with a colourful dusting of chilli.

5 Tip the popcorn into a large bowl and keep warm. Add a squeeze of lime juice immediately before serving.

Nutritional information per portion: Energy 741kcal/3085kJ; Protein 7.8g; Carbohydrate 60.9g, of which sugars 1.4g; Fat 53.5g, of which saturates 5.4g; Cholesterol 0mg; Calcium 13mg; Fibre 0g; Sodium 5mg.

Chicken flautas

Crisp fried tortillas with a chicken and cheese filling make a delicious light meal. Make sure that the oil is sufficiently hot to prevent the flutes from absorbing too much of it.

MAKES 12

2 skinless chicken breast fillets
15ml/1 tbsp vegetable oil
1 onion, finely chopped
2 garlic cloves, crushed
90g/3¹/₂ oz feta cheese, crumbled
12 corn tortillas, freshly made or a few
    days old
oil, for frying
salt and ground black pepper

FOR THE SALSA

3 tomatoes, peeled, seeded and chopped
juice of ¹/₂ lime
small bunch of fresh coriander (cilantro),
    chopped
¹/₂ small onion, finely chopped
3 fresh fresno chillies or similar fresh
    green chillies, seeded and chopped

1 Start by making the salsa. Mix the tomatoes, lime juice, coriander, onion and chillies in a bowl. Season with salt to taste and set aside.

2 Put the chicken breast fillets in a large pan, add water to cover and bring to the boil. Lower the heat and simmer for 15–20 minutes or until cooked. Remove the chicken and let cool a little. Shred into small pieces. Set aside.

3 Heat the oil in a frying pan, add the onion and garlic and fry over a low heat for 5 minutes, or until the onion has softened but not coloured. Add the chicken and season. Mix well, remove from the heat and stir in the feta.

4 Soften the tortillas by steaming 3 or 4 at a time on a plate over boiling water. Place a spoonful of the chicken filling on one of the tortillas. Roll up to make a cylinder and secure with a cocktail stick. Cover with clear film (plastic wrap) and fill and roll the remaining tortillas.

5 Pour oil into a frying pan to a depth of 2.5cm/1in. Heat it until a small cube of bread rises to the surface and bubbles at the edges before turning golden. Remove the cocktail sticks, then add the flutes to the pan, a few at a time. Fry for 2–3 minutes until golden, turning frequently. Drain on kitchen paper and serve at once, with the salsa.

Nutritional information per portion: Energy 131kcal/553kJ; Protein 9.6g; Carbohydrate 16.8g, of which sugars 1.9g; Fat 3.3g, of which saturates 1.4g; Cholesterol 23mg; Calcium 73mg; Fibre 1.2g; Sodium 209mg.

Molettes

Sold by street traders around mid-morning, this is perfect for a late breakfast.

SERVES 4

4 crusty finger rolls
50g/2oz/¼ cup butter, softened
225g/8oz/1⅓ cups refried beans
150g/5oz/1¼ cups grated medium Cheddar cheese
green salad leaves, to garnish
120ml/4fl oz/½ cup Classic Tomato Salsa, to serve

1 Cut the rolls in half, then take a sliver off the base so that they lie flat. Remove a little of the crumbs. Spread them lightly with enough butter to crisp.

2 Arrange them on a baking sheet and grill for about 5 minutes, or until they are crisp and golden. Meanwhile, heat the refried beans over a low heat in a small pan.

3 Scoop the beans into the rolls, then sprinkle the grated cheese on top. Pop back under the grill until the cheese melts. Serve with the tomato salsa and garnish with salad leaves.

Nutritional information per portion: Energy 446kcal/1868kJ; Protein 20.9g; Carbohydrate 40.8g, of which sugars 7g; Fat 22.2g, of which saturates 13.8g; Cholesterol 59mg; Calcium 460mg; Fibre 4.4g; Sodium 1091mg.

Eggs motulenos

This makes a tasty and filling breakfast or midday snack.

SERVES 4

225g/8oz/generous 1 cup black beans, soaked overnight in water
1 small onion, finely chopped
2 garlic cloves
small bunch of fresh coriander (cilantro), chopped
4 corn tortillas
30ml/2 tbsp oil
4 eggs
60ml/4 tbsp hot chilli sauce
75g/3oz feta cheese, crumbled
salt and ground black pepper
cooked peas, cooked ham and Classic Tomato Salsa, to serve

1 Drain the beans, rinse them under cold water and drain again. Put them in a pan, add the onion and garlic and water to cover. Bring to the boil, then simmer for 40 minutes. Stir in the coriander, season with salt and pepper to taste, and keep the beans hot.

2 Wrap the tortillas in foil. Place them on a plate over a pan of boiling water and steam for about 5 minutes. Alternatively, wrap them in microwave-safe film and heat them in a microwave on full power for 30 seconds.

3 Heat the oil in a frying pan and fry the eggs until the whites are set. Lift on to a plate and keep warm while you quickly heat the ham and peas in the remaining oil.

4 Top each tortilla with some beans. Place an egg on each tortilla, spoon over 15ml/1 tbsp hot chilli sauce, then surround each egg with some peas and ham. Sprinkle feta over the peas and serve with salsa.

Nutritional information per portion: Energy 423kcal/1773kJ; Protein 31g; Carbohydrate 36.1g, of which sugars 4.9g; Fat 18.4g, of which saturates 5.8g; Cholesterol 223mg; Calcium 178mg; Fibre 7.4g; Sodium 779mg.

Eggs with chorizo

Freshly made chorizo can be used in a number of savoury dishes, but is particularly good with scrambled egg, as here.

SERVES 4

25g/1oz/2 tbsp lard or white cooking fat
500g/1¼ lb minced (ground) pork
3 garlic cloves, crushed
10ml/2 tsp dried oregano
5ml/1 tsp ground cinnamon
2.5ml/½ tsp ground cloves
2.5ml/½ tsp ground black pepper
30ml/2 tbsp dry sherry
5ml/1 tsp caster (superfine) sugar
5ml/1 tsp salt
6 eggs
2 tomatoes, peeled, seeded and finely diced
½ small onion, finely chopped
60ml/4 tbsp milk or single (light) cream
fresh oregano sprigs, to garnish
warm corn or wheat flour tortillas, to serve

1 Melt the lard or fat in a frying pan over a moderate heat. Add the mince and cook until browned, stirring frequently. Stir in the garlic, dried oregano, cinnamon, cloves and black pepper. Cook for 3–4 minutes more.

2 Add the sherry, caster sugar and salt to the mince, stir well and cook for 3–4 minutes. Remove from the heat.

3 Put the eggs in a bowl. Beat lightly to mix, then stir in the tomatoes and onion. Return the chorizo mixture to the heat. Heat it through and pour in the egg mixture. Cook, stirring constantly, until the egg is almost firm. Stir in the milk or cream and check the seasoning. Garnish with fresh oregano and serve with tortillas.

Nutritional information per portion: Energy 399kcal/1665kJ; Protein 41g; Carbohydrate 6.4g, of which sugars 2.7g; Fat 22.7g, of which saturates 7.5g; Cholesterol 380mg; Calcium 137mg; Fibre 2.9g; Sodium 256mg.

Chillies in cheese sauce

This makes an excellent appetizer, light lunch or dip to serve with drinks. The chillies and tequila give it quite a kick.

SERVES 4–6

4 fresh fresno chillies or other fresh green chillies
15ml/1 tbsp vegetable oil
½ red onion, finely chopped
500g/1¼ lb/5 cups grated Monterey Jack cheese
30ml/2 tbsp crème fraîche
150ml/¼ pint/⅔ cup double (heavy) cream
2 firm tomatoes, peeled
15ml/1 tbsp reposada tequila
Tortilla Chips, to serve

1 Place the chillies in a dry frying pan over a moderate heat, turning them frequently until the skin blisters and darkens. Place the chillies in a strong plastic bag and tie the top to keep the steam in. Set aside for 20 minutes, then carefully peel off the skins. Slit the chillies and scrape out the seeds, then cut the flesh into thin strips. Cut these in half lengthways.

2 Heat the oil in a frying pan and fry the onion over a moderate heat for 5 minutes, until it is beginning to soften. Add the cheese, crème fraîche and cream. Stir over a low heat until the cheese melts and the mixture becomes a rich, creamy sauce. Stir in the thick chilli strips.

3 Cut the tomatoes in half and remove the seeds. Cut the flesh into 1cm/½ in pieces and stir these into the sauce.

4 Just before serving, stir in the tequila. Pour the sauce into a serving dish and serve warm, with the tortilla chips.

Nutritional information per portion: Energy 402kcal/1668kJ; Protein 21.8g; Carbohydrate 3.1g, of which sugars 2.8g; Fat 31.3g, of which saturates 19.7g; Cholesterol 86mg; Calcium 625mg; Fibre 0.7g; Sodium 608mg.

Eggs rancheros

There are many variations on this popular dish, which is great for breakfast or brunch. The combination of creamy eggs with onion, chilli and tomatoes works wonderfully well.

SERVES 4

2 corn tortillas, several days old
oil, for frying
2 fresh green jalapeño chillies
1 garlic clove
4 spring onions (scallions)
1 large tomato

8 eggs, beaten
150ml/¼ pint/²/₃ cup single
(light) cream
small bunch of fresh coriander (cilantro),
finely chopped
salt and ground black pepper

1 Cut the tortillas into long strips. Pour oil into a frying pan to a depth of 1cm/½ in. Heat the oil until very hot then fry the tortilla strips in batches for a minute or two until crisp and golden, turning occasionally. Drain on kitchen paper.

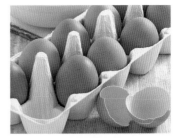

2 Spear the chillies on a long-handled metal skewer and roast them over the flame of a gas burner until the skins blister and darken. Do not let the flesh burn. Place them in a strong plastic bag and set aside for 20 minutes.

3 Meanwhile, crush the garlic and chop the spring onions finely. Cut a cross in the base of the tomato, place in a heatproof bowl and pour over boiling water to cover. After 3 minutes lift the tomato out and plunge into a bowl of cold water. Drain the tomato, remove the skin and quarter. Scoop out the seeds and the core, then dice the flesh finely.

4 Remove the chillies from the bag and peel off the skins. Cut off the stalks, then slit the chillies and scrape out the seeds. Chop the flesh. Put the eggs in a bowl, season and beat lightly.

5 Heat 15ml/1 tbsp oil in a pan. Add the garlic and spring onions and fry gently for 2–3 minutes until soft. Stir in the tomato and cook for 3–4 minutes, then stir in the chillies and cook for 1 minute.

6 Pour the eggs into the pan and stir until they start to set. When only a small amount of uncooked egg remains visible, stir in the cream. Stir the chopped coriander into the scrambled egg. Arrange the tortilla strips on four serving plates and spoon the eggs over. Serve at once.

Nutritional information per portion: Energy 307kcal/1281kJ; Protein 16.4g; Carbohydrate 17.2g, of which sugars 2.5g; Fat 20g, of which saturates 8.5g; Cholesterol 405mg; Calcium 151mg; Fibre 1.5g; Sodium 229mg.

Tortilla chips

Tortilla chips are used for scooping salsa or dips. Use tortillas that are a few days old; fresh ones will not crisp up so well.

SERVES 4

4–8 corn tortillas
oil, for frying
salt

1 Cut each tortilla into six triangular wedges. Pour oil into a large frying pan to a depth of 1cm/^{1}/$_2$ in, place the pan over a moderate heat and heat until very hot.

2 Fry the tortilla wedges in the hot oil in small batches until they turn golden and are crisp. This will only take a few moments. Remove with a slotted spoon and drain on kitchen paper. Sprinkle with salt.

3 Tortilla chips should be served warm. They can be cooled completely and stored in an airtight container for a few days, but will need to be reheated in a microwave or a warm oven before being served.

Nutritional information per portion: Energy 230kcal/964kJ; Protein 3.8g; Carbohydrate 30.1g, of which sugars 0.6g; Fat 11.3g, of which saturates 2g; Cholesterol 0mg; Calcium 75mg; Fibre 3g; Sodium 430mg.

Pepitas

These little snacks are absolutely irresistible, especially if you include chipotle chillies. Serve them with pre-dinner drinks.

SERVES 4

130g/4^1/$_2$ oz/1 cup pumpkin seeds
4 garlic cloves, crushed
1.5ml/^{1}/$_4$ tsp salt
10ml/2 tsp crushed dried chillies
5ml/1 tsp caster (superfine) sugar
a wedge of lime, to serve

1 Heat a small heavy frying pan, add the pumpkin seeds and dry fry for a few minutes, stirring them constantly as they swell.

2 When all the seeds have swollen, add the garlic and cook for a few minutes more, stirring all the time. Add the salt and the crushed chillies and stir to mix. Turn off the heat, but keep the pan on the stove. Sprinkle sugar over the seeds and shake the pan to ensure that they are all coated.

3 Tip the pepitas into a bowl and serve with the wedge of lime for squeezing over the seeds. If the lime is omitted, the seeds can be cooled and stored in an airtight container for reheating later, but they are best served fresh.

Nutritional information per portion: Energy 299kcal/1242kJ; Protein 10.3g; Carbohydrate 11.2g, of which sugars 2g; Fat 23.8g, of which saturates 2.3g; Cholesterol 0mg; Calcium 57mg; Fibre 3.2g; Sodium 2mg.

Fish and shellfish

With the Pacific Ocean and Gulf of Mexico

teeming with different varieties of fish, it

is no surprise that Mexican cooks produce

a marvellous range of seafood dishes. Some

of these recipes, such as prawns in garlic

butter, make simple after-work meals, while

others, such as salmon with tequila cream

sauce, are perfect for entertaining.

Salt cod for Christmas Eve

This Mexican dish is milder than the similar Spanish dish, Bacalao a la Vizcaina. *It is traditionally eaten on* Noche buena *or Christmas Eve throughout Mexico.*

SERVES 6

450g/1lb dried salt cod
105ml/7 tbsp extra virgin olive oil
1 onion, halved and thinly sliced
4 garlic cloves, crushed
2 x 400g/14oz cans chopped tomatoes
75g/3oz/¾ cup flaked (slivered) almonds
75g/3oz/½ cup pickled jalapeño
   chilli slices

115g/4oz/1 cup green olives stuffed
   with pimiento
small bunch of fresh parsley,
   finely chopped
salt and ground black pepper
fresh flat-leaf parsley, to garnish
crusty bread, to serve

1 Put the cod in a large bowl and pour over enough cold water to cover. Soak for 24 hours, changing the water at least five times during this period. Drain the cod and remove the skin using a large sharp knife. Shred the flesh finely using two forks, and put it into a bowl. Set it aside.

2 Heat half the oil in a frying pan. Add the onion slices and fry over a moderate heat until the onion is translucent. Remove the onion from the pan and set aside. Make sure you transfer the oil with the onion as it is an important flavouring in this dish and mustn't be discarded. In the same pan add the remaining olive oil. When the oil is hot but not smoking, add the garlic and fry for 2 minutes.

3 Add the canned tomatoes and their juice to the pan with the garlic. Cook over a medium-high heat for about 20 minutes, stirring occasionally, until the mixture has reduced and thickened.

4 Meanwhile, spread out the almonds in a single layer in a large heavy frying pan. Toast them over a moderate heat for a few minutes, shaking the pan lightly throughout the process so that they turn golden brown all over. Do not let them burn.

5 Add the chilli slices and stuffed olives to the toasted almonds. Stir in the shredded fish, mixing it in thoroughly, and cook for 20 minutes more, stirring occasionally, until the mixture is almost dry. Season to taste, add the parsley and cook for a further 2–3 minutes. Garnish with parsley leaves and serve in heated bowls, with crusty bread.

Nutritional information per portion: Energy 353kcal/1473kJ; Protein 29g; Carbohydrate 6.2g, of which sugars 5.5g; Fat 23.9g, of which saturates 2.8g; Cholesterol 44mg; Calcium 97mg; Fibre 3.6g; Sodium 881mg.

Ceviche

This famous dish is particularly popular along Mexico's western seaboard, in places such as Acapulco. It consists of very fresh raw fish, "cooked" by the action of lime juice.

SERVES 6

200g/7oz raw peeled prawns (shrimp)
200g/7oz shelled scallops
200g/7oz squid, cleaned and cut into
    serving pieces
7 limes
3 tomatoes
1 small onion
1 ripe avocado
20ml/4 tbsp chopped fresh oregano,
    or 10ml/2 tsp dried
5ml/1 tsp salt
ground black pepper
fresh oregano sprigs, to garnish
crusty bread and lime wedges, to serve
    (optional)

1 Spread out the prawns, scallops and squid in a non-metallic bowl. Squeeze six of the limes and pour the juice over the mixed seafood to cover it completely. Cover the dish with clear film (plastic wrap) and set aside for 8 hours or overnight.

2 Drain the seafood in a colander to remove the excess lime juice, then pat it dry with kitchen paper. Place the prawns, scallops and squid in a bowl.

3 Cut the tomatoes in half, squeeze out the seeds, then dice the flesh. Cut the onion in half, then slice it thinly. Cut the avocado in half lengthways, remove the stone and peel, then cut the flesh into 1cm/1/2 in dice.

4 Add the tomatoes, onion and avocado to the seafood with the oregano and seasoning. Squeeze the remaining lime and pour over the juice. Garnish with oregano and serve, with crusty bread and lime wedges, if liked.

Nutritional information per portion: Energy 147kcal/620kJ; Protein 21.9g; Carbohydrate 4.4g, of which sugars 2.2g; Fat 4.8g, of which saturates 1.1g; Cholesterol 175mg; Calcium 53mg; Fibre 1.2g; Sodium 186mg.

Escabeche

Escabeche is often confused with Ceviche, which consists of marinated raw fish. In Escabeche, the raw fish is initially marinated in lime juice, but is then cooked before being pickled.

SERVES 4

900g/2lb fish fillets
juice of 2 limes
300ml/¹/₂ pint/1¹/₄ cups olive oil
6 peppercorns
3 garlic cloves, sliced
2.5ml/¹/₂ tsp ground cumin
2.5ml/¹/₂ tsp dried oregano
2 bay leaves
50g/2oz/¹/₃ cup pickled jalapeño chilli
   slices, chopped
1 onion, thinly sliced
250ml/8fl oz/1 cup white wine vinegar
150g/5oz/1¹/₄ cups green olives stuffed
   with pimiento, to garnish

1 Place the fish fillets in a single layer in a shallow non-metallic dish. Pour the lime juice over, turn the fillets over once to ensure that they are completely coated, then cover the dish and leave to marinate for 15 minutes.

2 Drain the fish, then pat the fillets dry with kitchen paper. Heat 60ml/4 tbsp of the oil in a frying pan, add the fillets and sauté for 5–6 minutes, turning once, until they are golden brown. Transfer them to a shallow dish.

3 Heat 30ml/2 tbsp of the remaining oil in a frying pan. Add the pepper, garlic, ground cumin, oregano, bay leaves and jalapeños, and cook over a low heat for 2 minutes, then increase the heat, add the onion slices and vinegar and bring to the boil. Lower the heat and simmer for 4 minutes.

4 Remove the pan from the heat and add the remaining oil. Stir well, then pour the mixture over the fish. Leave to cool, then cover the dish and marinate for 24 hours in the fridge. To serve, drain off the liquid and garnish the fish with the stuffed olives.

Nutritional information per portion: Energy 414kcal/1720kJ; Protein 41.9g; Carbohydrate 1.3g, of which sugars 1g; Fat 26.7g, of which saturates 3.2g; Cholesterol 104mg; Calcium 30mg; Fibre 0.2g; Sodium 137mg.

Pueblo fish bake

The tangy lime juice is a perfect partner for the baked trout, which is an oily fish. Marinating means that the fish is beautifully tender and moist when cooked.

SERVES 4

2 fresh pasilla chillies

4 rainbow trout, cleaned

4 garlic cloves

10ml/2 tsp dried oregano

juice of 2 limes

50g/2oz/¹/₂ cup flaked (sliced) almonds

salt and ground black pepper

1 Roast the chillies in a dry frying pan or griddle pan until the skins are blistered, being careful not to let the flesh burn. Put them in a strong plastic bag and tie the top to keep the steam in. Set aside for 20 minutes.

2 Meanwhile, rub a little salt into the cavities in the trout, to ensure they are completely clean, then rinse them under cold running water. Drain and pat dry with kitchen paper.

3 Remove the chillies from the bag and peel off the skins. Cut off the stalks, then slit the chillies and scrape out the seeds. Chop the flesh roughly and put it in a mortar. Crush with a pestle until the mixture forms a paste.

4 Place the chilli paste in a shallow dish that will hold all the trout in a single layer. Slice the garlic lengthways and add to the dish. Add the oregano and 10ml/2 tsp salt, then stir in the lime juice and pepper to taste. Add the trout, turning to coat them in the mixture. Cover the dish and set aside for at least 30 minutes, turning the trout again halfway through.

5 Preheat the oven to 200°C/400°F/Gas 6. Have ready four pieces of foil, each large enough to wrap a trout. Top each sheet with a piece of greaseproof (waxed) paper of the same size. Place one trout on one of the pieces of paper, moisten with the marinade, then sprinkle a quarter of the almonds over the top. Bring up the sides of the paper and fold over to seal in the fish, then fold the foil over to make a neat parcel. Make three more parcels, then place side by side in a roasting pan.

6 Transfer the parcels to the oven and bake for 25 minutes. Put each parcel on an individual plate, or open them in the kitchen and serve unwrapped if you prefer.

Nutritional information per portion: Energy 236kcal/989kJ; Protein 27.2g; Carbohydrate 1.1g, of which sugars 0.8g; Fat 13.7g, of which saturates 1.8g; Cholesterol 77mg; Calcium 63mg; Fibre 1g; Sodium 64mg.

Veracruz-style red snapper

This is the most famous dish to come from the port of Veracruz. It borrows bay leaves and olives from Spain to go with the native chillies.

SERVES 4

4 whole red snapper, cleaned
juice of 2 limes
4 garlic cloves, crushed
5ml/1 tsp dried oregano
2.5ml/¹⁄₂ tsp salt
drained bottled capers, to garnish
lime wedges, to serve (optional)

FOR THE SAUCE

120ml/4fl oz/¹⁄₂ cup olive oil
2 bay leaves
2 garlic cloves, sliced
4 jalapeño chillies, seeded and cut in strips
1 onion, thinly sliced
8 fresh tomatoes
75g/3oz/¹⁄₂ cup pickled jalapeño chilli
    slices
15ml/1 tbsp soft dark brown sugar
2.5ml/¹⁄₂ tsp ground cloves
2.5ml/¹⁄₂ tsp ground cinnamon
150g/5oz/1¹⁄₄ cups green olives

1 Preheat the oven to 180°C/350°F/Gas 4. Rinse the fish inside and out. Pat dry with kitchen paper. Place in a roasting pan in a single layer.

2 Mix the lime juice, garlic, oregano and salt in a small bowl. Pour the mixture over the fish. Bake the fish for 30 minutes, or until the flesh flakes easily when tested with the tip of a sharp knife.

3 To make the sauce, heat the oil in a pan, add the bay leaves, garlic and chilli; fry over a low heat for 3–4 minutes. Add the onion slices to the oil in the pan and cook for 3–4 minutes, until all the onion is soft.

4 Cut a cross in the base of each tomato. Place them in a heatproof bowl and pour over boiling water to cover. After 3 minutes, plunge them into a bowl of cold water. Drain. Skin the tomatoes, cut them in half and squeeze out the seeds. Chop the flesh and add it to the onion mixture. Cook for 3 minutes, until the tomato is starting to soften.

5 Add the jalapeños, brown sugar, cloves and cinnamon to the sauce. Cook for 10 minutes, stirring often. Stir the olives into the sauce and pour a little over each fish. Garnish with the capers and serve with lime wedges, if liked.

Nutritional information per portion: Energy 421kcal/1757kJ; Protein 31.7g; Carbohydrate 11.4g, of which sugars 11.1g; Fat 28g, of which saturates 4.3g; Cholesterol 56mg; Calcium 106mg; Fibre 3.3g; Sodium 979mg.

Red snapper burritos

Fish makes a great filling for a tortilla, especially when it is succulent red snapper mixed with rice, chilli and tomatoes.

SERVES 6

3 red snapper fillets
90g/3¹/₂ oz/¹/₂ cup long grain white rice
30ml/2 tbsp vegetable oil
1 small onion, finely chopped
5ml/1 tsp ground achiote seed (annatto powder)
1 dried chilli, seeded and ground
75g/3oz/³/₄ cup flaked (sliced) almonds
200g/7oz can chopped tomatoes in tomato juice
150g/5oz/1¹/₄ cups grated Monterey Jack or mild Cheddar cheese
8 x 20cm/8in wheat flour tortillas
fresh flat-leaf parsley to garnish
lime wedges, to serve (optional)

1 Preheat the grill (broiler). Grill (broil) the red snapper fillets on an oiled rack for 5 minutes, turning the fish once. When cool, remove the skin and flake the fish into a bowl. Set it aside.

2 Put the rice in a pan, cover with cold water, cover and bring to the boil. Drain, rinse and drain again.

3 Heat the oil in a pan and fry the onion until soft and translucent. Stir in the ground achiote (annatto powder) and the chilli and cook for 5 minutes.

4 Add the rice, then stir in the fish and almonds. Add the tomatoes, with their juice. Cook over a moderate heat until the juice is absorbed and the rice is tender. Stir in the cheese and remove from the heat. Warm the tortillas.

5 Divide the filling among the tortillas, placing it in the centre of each one. Fold over the sides of each tortilla into the centre, then fold over the bottom to make a parcel. Garnish with parsley and serve with lime wedges, if liked.

Nutritional information per portion: Energy 484kcal/2033kJ; Protein 31.9g; Carbohydrate 54.7g, of which sugars 2.1g; Fat 15.9g, of which saturates 4.8g; Cholesterol 53mg; Calcium 262mg; Fibre 2.6g; Sodium 388mg.

Sea bass with orange chilli salsa

This aromatic citrus salsa has a tangy, mouthwatering freshness that provides a perfect contrast to the wonderful flavour of fresh sea bass.

SERVES 4

4 sea bass fillets
salt and ground black pepper
fresh coriander (cilantro), to garnish

FOR THE SALSA
2 fresh green chillies
2 oranges or pink grapefruit
1 small onion

1 Make the salsa. Roast the chillies in a dry griddle pan until the skins are blistered. Put them in a plastic bag and tie the top to keep the steam in. Set aside for 20 minutes.

2 Slice the top and bottom off each fruit and cut off all the peel and pith. Cut between the membranes and put each segment in a bowl.

3 Remove the chillies from the bag and peel off the skins. Cut off the stalks, then slit the chillies and scrape out the seeds. Chop the flesh finely. Cut the onion in half and slice it thinly. Add the onion and chillies to the orange pieces and mix lightly. Season and chill.

4 Season the sea bass fillets. Line a steamer with greaseproof (waxed) paper, allowing extra to enable the fish to be lifted out after cooking. Place the empty steamer over a pan of water and bring to the boil.

5 Place the fish in a single layer in the steamer. Cover and steam for about 8 minutes or until just cooked. Garnish with fresh coriander and serve with the salsa.

Nutritional information per portion: Energy 186kcal/783kJ; Protein 30.3g; Carbohydrate 7.7g, of which sugars 7.3g; Fat 3.9g, of which saturates 0.6g; Cholesterol 120mg; Calcium 238mg; Fibre 1.5g; Sodium 109mg.

Red snapper with coriander and almonds

Fish is often best when cooked plainly to preserve its freshness and flavour. This simple treatment is an ideal way of cooking red snapper, a fish that is very popular in Mexico.

SERVES 4

75g/3oz/³⁄₄ cup plain (all-purpose) flour
4 red snapper fillets
salt and ground black pepper
75g/3oz/6 tbsp butter
15ml/1 tbsp vegetable oil
75g/3oz/³⁄₄ cup flaked (sliced) almonds
grated rind and juice of 1 lime
small bunch of fresh coriander (cilantro),
    finely chopped
warm wheat flour tortillas, to serve

1 Preheat the oven to 140°C/ 275°F/Gas 1. Spread out the flour in a shallow dish and add seasoning. Dry the fish fillets with kitchen paper, then coat each fillet in the seasoned flour.

2 Heat the butter and oil in a frying pan. Add the snapper fillets, in batches if necessary, and cook for 2 minutes. Turn the fillets over carefully and cook the other side until golden.

3 Using a fish slice (metal spatula), carefully transfer the fillets to a shallow dish and keep them warm in the oven. Add the almonds to the fat remaining and fry them for 3–4 minutes, until golden.

4 Add the lime rind, juice and coriander to the almonds in the frying pan and stir well. Heat through for 1–2 minutes, then pour the mixture over the fish. Serve with warm wheat flour tortillas.

Nutritional information per portion: Energy 465kcal/1936kJ; Protein 25.8g; Carbohydrate 16.3g, of which sugars 1.5g; Fat 33.4g, of which saturates 13.2g; Cholesterol 85mg; Calcium 140mg; Fibre 2.6g; Sodium 221mg.

Swordfish tacos

This meaty fish is delicious and makes a great change from beef or chicken as a taco filling.It is important not to overcook it, or it can be dry.

SERVES 4
3 swordfish steaks
2 tbsp vegetable oil
2 garlic cloves
1 small onion, chopped
3 fresh green chiles, seeded and chopped
3 tomatoes
small bunch coriander (cilantro), chopped
6 fresh corn tortillas
1/2 iceberg lettuce, shredded
salt and ground black pepper
lemon wedges, to serve (optional)

1 Preheat the grill (broiler). Put the fish on an oiled rack over a grill pan and grill (broil) for 2–3 minutes on each side. When cool enough to handle, remove the skin and flake the fish into a bowl.

2 Heat the oil in a pan. Add the garlic, onion and chillies and fry for 5 minutes or until the onion is soft.

3 Cut a cross in the base of each tomato and pour over boiling water. After 3 minutes, plunge into cold water. Remove the skins and seeds and dice the flesh.

4 Add the tomatoes and swordfish to the onion mixture. Cook for 5 minutes over a low heat. Add the coriander and cook for 1–2 minutes. Season to taste.

5 Wrap the tortillas in foil and steam on a plate over boiling water until pliable. Place some lettuce and fish on each tortilla. Fold in half and serve with lemon wedges.

Nutritional information per portion: Energy 293kcal/1236kJ; Protein 22.7g; Carbohydrate 33.2g, of which sugars 3.7g; Fat 8.6g, of which saturates 1.4g; Cholesterol 41mg; Calcium 77mg; Fibre 2.1g; Sodium 276mg

Chargrilled swordfish

Swordfish is a prime candidate for the barbecue, as long as it is not overcooked. It tastes wonderful with this spicy sauce.

SERVES 4
2 fresh serrano chillies
4 tomatoes
45ml/3 tbsp olive oil
grated rind and juice of 1 lime
4 swordfish steaks
175ml/6fl oz/3/4 cup crème fraîche
salt and ground black pepper
fresh flat-leaf parsley, to garnish

1 Roast the chillies in a dry griddle pan until the skins are blistered. Put in a plastic bag and tie the top. Set aside for 20 minutes, then peel off the skins. Cut off the stalks, slit the chillies, remove the seeds and slice the flesh.

2 Cut a cross in the base of each tomato. Place them in a heatproof bowl and pour over boiling water to cover. After 3 minutes, plunge the tomatoes into a bowl of cold water. Drain. Remove the skins and seeds and chop the flesh into 1cm/1/2 in dice.

3 Heat 15ml/1 tbsp of the oil in a small pan and add the strips of chilli, with the lime rind and juice. Cook for 2–3 minutes, then stir in the tomatoes. Cook for 10 minutes, stirring occasionally, until the tomato is pulpy.

4 Brush the swordfish steaks with olive oil and season. Barbecue or grill for 3–4 minutes or until just cooked, turning once. Meanwhile, stir the crème fraîche into the sauce, heat it through gently and pour over the fish. Serve garnished with fresh parsley.

Nutritional information per portion: Energy 444kcal/1843kJ; Protein 28.8g; Carbohydrate 4.3g, of which sugars 4.2g; Fat 34.7g, of which saturates 16.2g; Cholesterol 118mg; Calcium 42mg; Fibre 1g; Sodium 215mg

Yucatán-style shark steak

A firm-fleshed fish, shark is widely available, either fresh or frozen. It needs careful watching, as overcooking will make it dry and tough, but the flavour is excellent.

SERVES 4

grated rind and juice of 1 orange
juice of 1 small lime
45ml/3 tbsp white wine
30ml/2 tbsp olive oil
2 garlic cloves, crushed
10ml/2 tsp ground achiote seed (annatto powder)
2.5ml/¹/₂ tsp cayenne pepper
2.5ml/¹/₂ tsp dried marjoram
5ml/1 tsp salt
4 shark steaks
fresh oregano leaves, to garnish
4 wheat flour tortillas and any suitable salsa, to serve

1 Put the orange rind and juice in a shallow non-metallic dish which is large enough to hold all the shark steaks in a single layer. Add the lime juice, white wine, olive oil, garlic, ground achiote (annatto powder), cayenne, marjoram and salt. Mix well.

2 Add the shark steaks to the dish and spoon the marinade over them. Cover and set aside for 1 hour, turning once.

3 Heat a griddle pan until very hot and cook the marinated shark steaks for 2–3 minutes on each side. Alternatively, they are very good cooked on the barbecue, so long as they are cooked after the coals have lost their fierce initial heat. Do not overcook.

4 Garnish the shark steaks with oregano and serve with the tortillas and a salsa. A green vegetable would also go well.

Nutritional information per portion: Energy 222kcal/931kJ; Protein 35g; Carbohydrate 1.4g, of which sugars 0.1g; Fat 7.7g, of which saturates 1g; Cholesterol 66mg; Calcium 60mg; Fibre 1.2g; Sodium 233mg.

Salmon with tequila cream sauce

Use reposada tequila, which is lightly aged, for this sauce. It has a smoother, more rounded flavour, which goes well with the cream.

SERVES 4

3 fresh jalapeño chillies
45ml/3 tbsp olive oil
1 small onion, finely chopped
150ml/¼ pint/⅔ cup fish stock
grated rind and juice of 1 lime
120ml/4fl oz/½ cup single (light) cream
30ml/2 tbsp reposada tequila
1 firm avocado
4 salmon fillets
salt and ground white pepper
strips of green pepper and fresh flat-leaf
    parsley, to garnish

1 Roast the chillies in a frying pan until the skins are blistered. Put them in a plastic bag and tie the top to keep the steam in. Set aside for 20 minutes.

2 Heat 15ml/1 tbsp of the oil in a pan. Add the onion and fry for 3–4 minutes, then add the stock, lime rind and juice. Cook for 10 minutes, until the stock reduces. Peel off the chilli skins, slit and scrape out the seeds.

3 Stir the cream into the onion mixture. Slice the chillies into strips and add to the pan. Cook over a gentle heat, stirring, for 2–3 minutes. Season. Stir in the tequila. Leave the pan over a very low heat. Peel the avocado, remove the stone and slice the flesh. Brush the fish on one side with a little of the oil.

4 Heat a frying pan or ridged grill pan (broiler) until very hot and add the salmon, oiled side down. Cook for 2–3 minutes, then brush the top with oil, turn each fillet over and cook until the fish flakes. Serve on a pool of sauce, with the avocado slices. Garnish with strips of green pepper and fresh parsley.

Nutritional information per portion: Energy 2895kcal/12052kJ; Protein 304.5g; Carbohydrate 2.3g, of which sugars 1.6g; Fat 183.1g, of which saturates 33.7g; Cholesterol 764mg; Calcium 345mg; Fibre 1.1g; Sodium 685mg.

Fried sole with lime

Simple fish dishes like this one capitalize on the delicious flavour of good fresh fish.

SERVES 4

75g/3oz/3/4 cup plain (all-purpose) flour
10ml/2 tsp garlic salt
5ml/1 tsp ground black pepper
4 sole fillets
oil, for frying
juice of 2 limes
small bunch of fresh parsley, chopped, plus extra sprigs
   to garnish
fresh salsa, to serve

1 Mix the flour, garlic salt and pepper together. Spread out the seasoned flour mixture in a shallow dish. Pat the sole fillets dry with kitchen paper, then turn them in the seasoned flour until they are evenly coated.

2 Pour oil into a wide frying pan to a depth of 2.5cm/1/2in. Heat it until a cube of bread added to the oil rises to the surface and browns in 45–60 seconds.

3 Add the fish, in batches if necessary, and fry for 3–4 minutes. Lift each fillet out and drain it on kitchen paper. Transfer to a heated serving dish.

4 Squeeze the juice of half a lime over each piece of fish and sprinkle with the chopped parsley. Serve immediately, with a fresh salsa to complement the fish. Garnish with parsley. New potatoes also go well.

Nutritional information per portion: Energy 444kcal/1843kJ; Protein 28.8g; Carbohydrate 4.3g, of which sugars 4.2g; Fat 34.7g, of which saturates 16.2g; Cholesterol 118mg; Calcium 42mg; Fibre 1g; Sodium 215mg.

Salmon with guavas

Guavas have a creamy flesh with a slight citrus tang and are perfect to serve with salmon.

SERVES 4

6 ripe guavas
45ml/3 tbsp vegetable oil
1 small onion, finely chopped
120ml/4fl oz/1/2 cup well-flavoured chicken stock
10ml/2 tsp hot pepper sauce
4 salmon steaks
salt and ground black pepper
strips of red pepper, to garnish

1 Cut each guava in half. Scoop the seeded soft flesh into a sieve placed over a bowl. Press it through the sieve, discard the seeds and skin and set the pulp aside.

2 Heat 30ml/2 tbsp of the oil in a frying pan. Fry the onion for about 4 minutes over a moderate heat until softened. Stir in the guava pulp, with the chicken stock and hot pepper sauce. Cook, stirring constantly, until the sauce thickens. Keep it warm until needed.

3 Brush the steaks on one side with a little of the oil. Season with salt and pepper. Heat a griddle or ridged grill (broiler) pan until very hot and add the steaks, oiled side down. Cook for 2–3 minutes, until the underside is golden, then brush the surface with oil, turn each steak over and cook the other side until the fish is cooked and flakes easily when tested with the tip of a knife.

4 Transfer each steak to a warmed plate. Serve, garnished with strips of red pepper on a pool of sauce. A fresh green salad is a good accompaniment.

Nutritional information per portion: Energy 1060kcal/4378kJ; Protein 31.5g; Carbohydrate 7.9g, of which sugars 7.5g; Fat 100.5g, of which saturates 12.6g; Cholesterol 75mg; Calcium 53mg; Fibre 5.2g; Sodium 76mg.

Prawns with almond sauce

The addition of ground almonds gives an interesting texture to the deliciously creamy, piquant sauce that accompanies these prawns.

SERVES 6

1 ancho or similar dried chilli
30ml/2 tbsp vegetable oil
1 onion, chopped
3 garlic cloves, roughly chopped
8 tomatoes
5ml/1 tsp ground cumin
120ml/4fl oz/1/2 cup chicken stock
130g/41/2 oz 1 cup ground almonds

175ml/6fl oz/3/4 cup crème fraîche
1/2 lime
900g/2lb cooked peeled prawns (shrimp)
salt
fresh coriander (cilantro) and spring
   onion (scallion) strips, to garnish
cooked rice and warm tortillas, to serve

1 Place the dried chilli in a heatproof bowl and pour over boiling water to cover. Leave to soak for 30 minutes. Drain, remove the stalk, then slit the chilli and scrape out the seeds. Chop the flesh roughly and set it aside. Heat the oil in a frying pan and fry the onion and garlic until soft.

2 Cut a cross in each tomato base. Place in a heatproof bowl and pour over boiling water. After 3 minutes, lift them out and plunge into a bowl of cold water. Drain. Skin the tomatoes, then cut in half and scoop out the seeds. Chop into 1cm/1/2 in cubes and add to the onion mixture, with the chilli. Stir in the ground cumin and cook for 10 minutes, stirring occasionally. Tip the mixture into a food processor, add the stock and process until smooth.

3 Pour the mixture into a large pan, add the ground almonds and stir over a low heat for 2–3 minutes. Stir in the crème fraîche until is has been incorporated completely.

4 Squeeze the juice from the lime and stir it into the sauce. Season with salt to taste, then increase the heat and bring the sauce to simmering point. Add the prawns and heat for 2–3 minutes, depending on size, until warmed through. Serve on a bed of rice and offer warm tortillas separately.

Nutritional information per portion: Energy 236kcal/989kJ; Protein 27.8g; Carbohydrate 5.3g, of which sugars 5.1g; Fat 11.7g, of which saturates 5.2g; Cholesterol 311mg; Calcium 140mg; Fibre 1.5g; Sodium 301mg.

Prawn salad

In Mexico, this salad would form the fish course in a formal meal, but it is so good that you'll want to serve it on all sorts of occasions. It is perfect for a buffet lunch.

SERVES 4

450g/1lb cooked peeled prawns (shrimp)
juice of 1 lime
3 tomatoes
1 ripe but firm avocado
30ml/2 tbsp hot chilli sauce
5ml/1 tsp sugar
150ml/¼ pint/²⁄₃ cup sour cream
2 Little Gem (Bibb) lettuces, separated
    into leaves
salt and ground black pepper
fresh basil leaves and strips of green
    (bell) pepper, to garnish

1 Put the prawns in a large bowl, add the lime juice and salt and pepper. Toss lightly, then leave to marinate.

2 Cut a cross in the base of each tomato. Place them in a bowl and pour over boiling water to cover.

3 After 3 minutes, lift the tomatoes out on a slotted spoon and plunge them into a bowl of cold water. Drain. The skins will have begun to peel back easily from the crosses.

4 Skin the tomatoes completely, then cut them in half and squeeze out the seeds. Chop the flesh into 1cm/½ in cubes and add it to the prawns.

5 Cut the avocado in half, remove the skin and seed, then slice the flesh into 1cm/½ in chunks. Add it to the prawn and tomato mixture.

6 Mix the hot chilli sauce, sugar and soured cream in a bowl. Fold into the prawn mixture. Line a bowl with the lettuce leaves, then top with the prawn mixture. Cover and chill for at least 1 hour, then garnish with fresh basil and strips of green pepper. Serve with crusty bread.

Nutritional information per portion: Energy 240kcal/1001kJ; Protein 24.3g; Carbohydrate 5.7g, of which sugars 5.4g; Fat 13.4g, of which saturates 6g; Cholesterol 266mg; Calcium 149mg; Fibre 1.8g; Sodium 262mg.

Prawns in garlic butter

This quick and easy dish is perfect for serving to friends who don't mind getting their hands dirty. Provide a plate for the prawn shells and offer warm tortillas for mopping up the juices.

SERVES 6

900g/2lb large raw tiger prawns (shrimp), in their shells, thawed if frozen
115g/4oz/¹/₂ cup butter
15ml/1 tbsp vegetable oil
6 garlic cloves, crushed
grated rind and juice of 2 limes
small bunch of fresh coriander (cilantro), chopped
warm tortillas, to serve
lemon slices, for the finger bowls

1 Rinse the prawns in a colander, remove their heads and leave them to drain. Heat the butter and oil in a large frying pan, add the garlic and fry over a low heat for 2–3 minutes.

2 Add the lime rind and juice. Cook, stirring the mixture constantly, for a further minute.

3 Add the prawns and cook them for 2–3 minutes until they turn pink. Remove from the heat, sprinkle with coriander and serve with the warm tortillas. Give each guest a finger bowl filled with water and a slice of lemon, for cleaning their fingers after shelling the prawns, and provide paper napkins.

Nutritional information per portion: Energy 156kcal/645kJ; Protein 13.7g; Carbohydrate 1.4g, of which sugars 0.4g; Fat 10.6g, of which saturates 5.3g; Cholesterol 66mg; Calcium 102mg; Fibre 0.7g; Sodium 974mg.

Crab with green rice

This is a popular dish in the western coastal areas of Mexico. Prawns can be used instead of crab meat if you prefer and the dish also works well with warm corn tortillas.

SERVES 4

225g/8oz/generous 1 cup long grain
   white rice
500g/1¼ lb/3⅓ cups drained canned
   tomatillos
large bunch of fresh coriander (cilantro)
1 onion, roughly chopped
3 poblano or other fresh green chillies,
   seeded and chopped
3 garlic cloves
45ml/3 tbsp olive oil
500g/1¼ lb crab meat
300ml/½ pint/1¼ cups fish stock
60ml/4 tbsp dry white wine
salt
sliced spring onions (scallions), to garnish

1 Put the rice in a heatproof bowl, pour over boiling water to cover and leave to stand for 20 minutes. Drain thoroughly.

2 Put the tomatillos in a food processor or blender and process until smooth. Chop half the coriander and add to the tomatillo purée, with the onion, chillies and garlic. Process again until smooth.

3 Heat the oil in a large pan. Add the rice and fry over a moderate heat for 5 minutes, until all the oil has been absorbed. Stir occasionally to prevent the rice from sticking.

4 Stir in the tomatillo mixture, with the crab meat, stock and wine. Cover and cook over a low heat for about 20 minutes or until all the liquid has been absorbed. Stir occasionally and add a little more liquid if the rice starts to stick to the pan. Add salt as required, then spoon into a dish and garnish with the remaining coriander and the sliced spring onions.

Nutritional information per portion: Energy 336kcal/1403kJ; Protein 16.3g; Carbohydrate 44.4g, of which sugars 4.1g; Fat 9.2g, of which saturates 1.4g; Cholesterol 45mg; Calcium 100mg; Fibre 1.2g; Sodium 355mg.

Scallops with garlic and coriander

Shellfish is often cooked very simply in Mexico and hot chilli sauce and lime are commonly used ingredients in many fish recipes.

SERVES 4

20 scallops
2 courgettes (zucchini)
75g/3oz/6 tbsp butter
15ml/1 tbsp vegetable oil
4 garlic cloves, chopped
30ml/2 tbsp hot chilli sauce
juice of 1 lime
small bunch of fresh coriander (cilantro),
    finely chopped

1 If you have bought scallops in their shells, open them. Hold a scallop shell in the palm of your hand, with the flat side uppermost. Insert the blade of a knife close to the hinge that joins the shells and prise them apart. Run the blade of the knife across the inside of the flat shell to cut away the scallop. Only the white adductor muscle and the orange coral are eaten, so pull away and discard all other parts. Rinse the scallops under cold running water.

2 Cut the courgettes in half, then into four pieces. Melt the butter in the oil in a large frying pan. Add the courgettes and fry until soft. Remove from the pan. Add the garlic and fry until golden. Stir in the hot chilli sauce.

3 Add the scallops to the sauce. Cook, stirring constantly, for 1–2 minutes only. Stir in the lime juice, chopped coriander and the courgette pieces. Serve immediately on heated plates.

Nutritional information per portion: Energy 278kcal/1151kJ; Protein 13.7g; Carbohydrate 5.8g, of which sugars 3.9g; Fat 22.4g, of which saturates 12.4g; Cholesterol 71mg; Calcium 45mg; Fibre 1g; Sodium 350mg.

Fisherman's stew

This is just the sort of hearty one-pot meal you can imagine fishermen cooking for themselves, using freshly caught fish and a few herbs and vegetables.

SERVES 6

500g/1¼ lb mussels
3 onions
2 garlic cloves, sliced
300ml/½ pint/1¼ cups fish stock
12 scallops
450g/1lb cod fillet
30ml/2 tbsp olive oil
1 large potato, about 200g/7oz
few sprigs of fresh thyme, chopped

1 red and 1 green (bell) pepper
120ml/4fl oz/½ cup dry white wine
250ml/8fl oz/1 cup crème fraîche
275g/10oz raw peeled prawns (shrimp)
75g/3oz/¾ cup grated mature (sharp)
    Cheddar cheese
salt and ground black pepper
fresh thyme sprigs, to garnish

1 Clean the mussel shells, removing any beards. Discard any that stay open when tapped. Rinse in cold water.

2 Pour water to a depth of 2.5cm/1in into a large, deep frying pan. Chop one onion and add it to the pan with the sliced garlic. Bring to the boil, then add the mussels and cover the pan tightly.

3 Cook the mussels for 5–6 minutes, shaking the pan occasionally. Remove them as they open, discarding any that remain shut. Remove the mussels from their shells and set them aside.

4 Strain the cooking liquid from the mussels through a muslin-lined sieve to remove any remaining sand. Make up the liquid with fish stock to 300ml/½ pint/1¼ cups.

5 If you have bought scallops in their shells, open them: hold a scallop shell in the palm of your hand, with the flat side uppermost. Insert the blade of a knife close to the hinge that joins the shells and prise apart. Run the blade of the knife across the inside of the flat shell to cut away the scallop. Only the white adductor muscle and the orange coral are eaten, so pull away and discard all other parts. Rinse the scallops under cold running water to remove any grit or sand, then put them in a bowl and set them aside.

6 Cut the cod into large cubes and put it in a bowl. Season with salt and pepper and set aside.

7 Cut the remaining onions into small wedges. Heat the olive oil in a large pan and fry the onion wedges for 2–3 minutes. Slice the potato about 1cm/$^1/_2$ in thick and add to the pan, with the fresh chopped thyme. Cover and cook for about 15 minutes, until the potato has softened.

8 Core the peppers, remove the cores and seeds, then dice the flesh. Add to the onion and potato mixture and cook for a few minutes. Stir in the mixed mussel and fish stock, with the wine and crème fraîche.

9 Bring to just below boiling point, then add the cod and scallops. Lower the heat and simmer for 5 minutes, then add the prawns. Simmer for a few minutes more, until all the seafood is cooked. Stir in the mussels and warm through for 1–2 minutes. Season the sauce. Spoon into bowls, garnish with the thyme sprigs and sprinkle with the cheese. Crusty bread would be an ideal accompaniment.

Nutritional information per portion: Energy 450kcal/1876kJ; Protein 39g; Carbohydrate 16.2g, of which sugars 6.2g; Fat 24.2g, of which saturates 13.4g; Cholesterol 206mg; Calcium 273mg; Fibre 1.7g; Sodium 370mg.

Poultry and meat

Pork is undoubtedly the most popular meat in Mexico. Every part of the animal is processed for food, so it represents terrific value for money. Turkey was popular in pre-Columbian times and still features on the menu today, although chicken is widely used for everyday dishes. Beef is popular in the north, and lamb and kid are also used.

Chicken fajitas

The perfect dish for casual entertaining, fajitas are flour tortillas that are brought to the table freshly cooked. Guests add their own fillings before folding the tortillas and tucking in.

SERVES 6

3 skinless chicken breast fillets
finely grated rind and juice of 2 limes
30ml/2 tbsp caster (superfine) sugar
10ml/2 tsp dried oregano
2.5ml/1/2 tsp cayenne pepper
5ml/1 tsp ground cinnamon
3 (bell) peppers (1 red, 1 yellow or orange
    and 1 green), cored, seeded and cut
    into 1cm/1/2in wide strips
45ml/3 tbsp vegetable oil

2 onions, thinly sliced
guacamole, salsa and sour cream, to serve

FOR THE TORTILLAS
250g/9oz/2¼ cups plain (all-purpose)
    flour, sifted
1.5ml/1/4 tsp baking powder
pinch of salt
50g/2oz/1/4 cup lard
60ml/4 tbsp warm water

1 Slice the chicken fillets into 2cm/3/4in wide strips and place these in a large bowl. Add the lime rind and juice, sugar, oregano, cayenne and cinnamon. Mix thoroughly. Set aside to marinate for at least 30 minutes.

2 Meanwhile, make the tortillas. Mix the flour, baking powder and salt in a large bowl. Rub in the lard, then add the warm water, a little at a time, to make a stiff dough. Knead this on a lightly floured surface for 10–15 minutes until it is smooth and elastic.

3 Divide the dough into 12 small balls, then roll each ball to a 15cm/6in round. Cover the rounds with plastic film to keep them from drying out.

4 Heat a frying pan and cook each tortilla in turn for about 1 minute on each side, or until the surface colours and begins to blister. Wrap the tortillas in a clean, dry dishtowel.

5 Heat the oil in a frying pan. Stir-fry the marinated chicken for 5–6 minutes, then add the peppers and onions and cook for 3–4 minutes more, until the chicken strips are cooked through and the vegetables are soft and tender, but still juicy. To serve, spread a little salsa onto a tortilla, add a spoonful of guacamole, pile some of the chicken mixture in the centre and add a small dollop of sour cream, then fold the tortilla.

Nutritional information per portion: Energy 485kcal/2044kJ; Protein 26g; Carbohydrate 67.4g, of which sugars 15.3g; Fat 14.2g, of which saturates 3.8g; Cholesterol 60mg; Calcium 118mg; Fibre 4g; Sodium 53mg.

Chicken with chipotle sauce

It is important to seek out chipotle chillies for this recipe, as they impart a wonderfully rich and smoky flavour to the chicken – you can use more than the quantity given if you wish. The purée can be made ahead of time, making this a very easy recipe for entertaining.

SERVES 6

6 chipotle chillies
200ml/7fl oz/scant 1 cup water
chicken stock (for quantity, see method)
3 onions

6 chicken breast fillets
45ml/3 tbsp vegetable oil
salt and ground black pepper
fresh oregano, to garnish

1 Put the dried chillies in a bowl and pour over hot water to cover. Leave to stand for about 30 minutes until very soft. Drain, reserving the soaking water in a measuring jug. Cut off the stalk from each chilli, then slit them lengthways and scrape out the seeds with a small sharp knife.

2 Preheat the oven to 180°C/350°F/Gas 4. Chop the flesh of the chillies roughly and put it in a food processor or blender. Add enough chicken stock to the soaking water to make it up to 400ml/14fl oz/1²/₃ cups. Pour it into the processor or blender and process at maximum power until smooth.

3 Peel the onions. Using a sharp knife, cut them in half, then slice them thinly. Separate the slices. Heat the oil in a large frying pan, add the onions and cook over a low to moderate heat for about 5 minutes, or until they have softened but not coloured, stirring occasionally. Meanwhile, remove the skin from the chicken breast fillets and trim off any stray pieces of fat or membrane.

4 Using a slotted spoon, transfer the onion slices to a casserole that is large enough to hold all the chicken breasts in a single layer.

5 Arrange the chicken fillets on top of the onion slices. Sprinkle with a little salt and several grindings of black pepper. Pour the chipotle purée over the chicken fillets, making sure that each piece is evenly coated.

6 Place the casserole in the preheated oven and bake for 45 minutes to 1 hour or until the chicken is cooked through, but is still moist and tender. Garnish with fresh oregano and serve with boiled white rice and Frijoles de Olla.

Nutritional information per portion: Energy 234kcal/984kJ; Protein 37.1g; Carbohydrate 5.3g, of which sugars 3.8g; Fat 7.3g, of which saturates 1.1g; Cholesterol 105mg; Calcium 27mg; Fibre 0.9g; Sodium 93mg.

Drunken chicken

Tequila is this chicken's tipple, and the dish has a delicious sweet-and-sour flavour. Serve it with green or yellow rice and flour tortillas to mop up the sauce.

SERVES 4

150g/5oz/scant 1 cup raisins
120ml/4fl oz/¹/₂ cup sherry
115g/4oz/1 cup plain (all-purpose) flour
2.5ml/¹/₂ tsp salt
2.5ml/¹/₂ tsp ground black pepper
45ml/3 tbsp vegetable oil
8 skinless chicken thighs, bone-in
1 onion, halved and thinly sliced
3 garlic cloves, crushed
2 tart eating apples, such as Granny
  Smith, peeled, cored and diced
115g/4oz/1 cup flaked (sliced) almonds
1 ripe plantain, peeled and sliced
350ml/12fl oz/1¹/₂ cups well-flavoured
  chicken stock
250ml/8fl oz/1 cup tequila
fresh herbs, chopped, to garnish
  (optional)

1 Put the raisins in a bowl and pour the sherry over. Set aside to plump up. Season the flour and spread it out on a large, flat dish.

2 Heat 30ml/2 tbsp of the oil in a large frying pan. Dip each chicken thigh in turn in the seasoned flour, then fry in the hot oil until browned, turning occasionally. Drain on kitchen paper.

3 Heat the remaining oil in a deep frying pan. Add the onion and garlic and cook for 2–3 minutes. Add the apple to the onion mixture with the almonds and plantain. Cook, stirring occasionally, for 3–4 minutes, then add the soaked raisins, with any free sherry. Add the chicken to the pan.

4 Pour the stock and tequila over the chicken. Cover the pan and cook for 15 minutes, then uncover and cook for 10 minutes more or until the sauce has reduced by half. Check that the thighs are cooked by lifting one out and piercing it in the thickest part with a sharp knife or skewer. Any juices that come out should be clear. Serve sprinkled with fresh herbs, if desired.

Nutritional information per portion: Energy 912kcal/3829kJ; Protein 53g; Carbohydrate 79g, of which sugars 43.4g; Fat 26.4g, of which saturates 2.8g; Cholesterol 123mg; Calcium 160mg; Fibre 5.5g; Sodium 145mg.

Chicken and tomatillo chimichangas

These fried burritos are a common sight on street stalls and in cafés along the Mexican border with Texas, but are not so well known further south.

SERVES 4

2 skinless chicken breast fillets
1 chipotle chilli, seeded
15ml/1 tbsp vegetable oil
2 onions, finely chopped
4 garlic cloves, crushed
2.5ml/½ tsp ground cumin
2.5ml/½ tsp ground coriander
2.5ml/½ tsp ground cinnamon
2.5ml/½ tsp ground cloves
300g/11oz/scant 2 cups drained canned
   tomatillos
400g/14oz/2⅓ cups cooked pinto beans
8 x 20–25cm/8–10in fresh wheat flour
   tortillas
oil, for frying
salt and ground black pepper

1 Put the chicken fillets in a large pan, pour over water to cover and add the chilli. Bring to the boil, lower the heat and simmer for 10 minutes or until the chilli has softened and the chicken is cooked. Remove and chop the chilli. Transfer the chicken to a plate. Leave to cool slightly, then shred.

2 Heat the oil in a frying pan. Fry the onions until translucent, then add the garlic and spices and cook for 3 minutes more. Add the tomatillos and beans. Cook over a moderate heat for 5 minutes, stirring constantly. Simmer gently for 5 minutes more. Add the chicken and seasoning.

3 Wrap the tortillas in foil and place them on a plate. Stand the plate over boiling water for 5 minutes until they are pliable.

4 Spoon one-eighth of the filling into the centre of a tortilla, fold in both sides and then the top and bottom. Secure with a cocktail stick.

5 Heat the oil in a frying pan and fry the chimichangas in batches until crisp, turning once. Remove them from the oil, drain on kitchen paper and serve.

Nutritional information per portion: Energy 613kcal/2579kJ; Protein 38g; Carbohydrate 69.7g, of which sugars 8.9g; Fat 22.2g, of which saturates 3.8g; Cholesterol 70mg; Calcium 237mg; Fibre 13.1g; Sodium 1123mg.

Burritos with chicken and rice

In Mexico, burritos are a popular street food, eaten on the hoof. The secret of a successful burrito is to have all the filling neatly packaged inside the tortilla for easy eating, so these snacks are seldom served with a pour-over sauce.

SERVES 4

90g/3¹/₂ oz/¹/₂ cup long grain rice
15ml/1 tbsp vegetable oil
1 onion, chopped
2.5ml/¹/₂ tsp ground cloves
5ml/1 tsp dried, or fresh oregano
200g/7oz can chopped tomatoes in
    tomato juice
2 skinless chicken breast fillets

150g/5oz/1¹/₄ cups grated Monterey Jack
    or mild Cheddar cheese
60ml/4 tbsp sour cream (optional)
8 x 20–25cm/8–10in fresh wheat flour
    tortillas
salt
fresh oregano, to garnish (optional)

1 Bring a pan of lightly salted water to the boil. Add the rice and cook for 8 minutes. Drain, rinse and then drain again.

2 Heat the oil in a large pan. Add the onion, with the ground cloves and oregano, and fry for 2–3 minutes. Stir in the rice and tomatoes and cook over a low heat until all the tomato juice has been absorbed. Set the pan aside.

3 Put the chicken in a pan, pour in water to cover and bring to the boil. Lower the heat and simmer for 10 minutes or until the chicken is cooked through. Lift the chicken out of the pan, put on a plate and cool slightly.

4 Preheat the oven to 160°C/325°F/Gas 3. Shred the chicken by pulling the flesh apart with two forks, then add the chicken to the rice mixture, with the cheese. Stir in the sour cream, if using.

5 Wrap the tortillas in foil and place them on a plate. Stand the plate over boiling water for 5 minutes. Alternatively, wrap in microwave-safe film and heat in a microwave for 1 minute.

6 Spoon one-eighth of the filling into the centre of a tortilla and fold in both sides. Fold the bottom up and the top down to form a parcel. Secure with a cocktail stick (toothpick). Put the filled burrito in a shallow dish, cover with foil and keep warm in the oven while you make seven more. Remove the cocktail sticks before serving, and serve sprinkled with fresh oregano, if liked.

Nutritional information per portion: Energy 626kcal/2634kJ; Protein 37.1g; Carbohydrate 82.4g, of which sugars 3.5g; Fat 17.2g, of which saturates 8.7g; Cholesterol 89mg; Calcium 403mg; Fibre 3.1g; Sodium 601mg.

Turkey mole

A mole is a rich stew, traditionally served on a festive occasion. The word comes from the Aztec "molli", meaning a chilli-flavoured sauce. This recipe features cocoa powder.

SERVES 4

1 ancho chilli, seeded
1 guajillo chilli, seeded
115g/4oz/³/4 cup sesame seeds
50g/2oz/¹/2 cup whole blanched almonds
50g/2oz/¹/2 cup shelled unsalted
    peanuts, skinned
1 small onion, finely chopped
2 garlic cloves, finely chopped
60ml/4 tbsp vegetable oil
50g/2oz/¹/3 cup canned tomatoes in
    tomato juice

1 ripe plantain
50g/2oz/¹/3 cup raisins
75g/3oz/¹/2 cup ready-to-eat prunes,
    pitted
5ml/1 tsp dried oregano
2.5ml/¹/2 tsp ground cloves
2.5ml/¹/2 tsp crushed allspice berries
5ml/1 tsp ground cinnamon
25g/1oz/¹/4 cup unsweetened cocoa powder
4 turkey breast steaks
fresh oregano, to garnish (optional)

1 Soak the chillies in a bowl of hot water for 30 minutes, then lift out and chop roughly. Reserve 250ml/8fl oz/1 cup of the soaking liquid.

2 Toast the sesame seeds in a frying pan over a moderate heat. Set aside 45ml/3 tbsp of the seeds for the garnish and tip the rest into a bowl. Toast the almonds and peanuts and add to the bowl. Heat half the vegetable oil in a frying pan, cook the onion and garlic for 2–3 minutes, then add the chillies and tomatoes. Cook gently for 10 minutes.

3 Peel the plantain and slice diagonally. Add to the onion mixture with the raisins, prunes, dried oregano, spices and cocoa. Stir in the reserved chilli water. Bring to the boil, stirring, then add the sesame seeds, almonds and peanuts. Cook for 10 minutes, stirring frequently, then remove from the heat and allow to cool slightly. Blend the sauce in batches in a food processor until smooth.

4 Heat the remaining lard or oil in a casserole. Add the turkey and brown over a moderate heat. Pour the sauce over and cover the casserole with foil and a lid. Cook over a gentle heat for 20–25 minutes. Sprinkle with the reserved sesame seeds and oregano, and serve with rice and tortillas.

Nutritional information per portion: Energy 710kcal/2977kJ; Protein 63g; Carbohydrate 36.7g, of which sugars 26.1g; Fat 35.7g, of which saturates 5.5g; Cholesterol 111mg; Calcium 219mg; Fibre 6.4g; Sodium 232mg.

Pork in green sauce with cactus

Chile Verde is a classic sauce. The inclusion of cactus pieces gives this dish an intriguing flavour which will doubtless prove a good talking point at the dinner table.

SERVES 4

30ml/2 tbsp vegetable oil
500g/1¼ lb pork shoulder, cut in
    2.5cm/1in cubes
1 onion, finely chopped
2 garlic cloves, crushed
5ml/1 tsp dried oregano
3 fresh jalapeño chillies, seeded and
    chopped
300g/11oz/scant 2 cups drained canned
    tomatillos
150ml/¼ pint/²⁄₃ cup vegetable stock
300g/11oz jar *nopalitos*, drained
salt and ground black pepper
warm fresh corn tortillas, to serve

1 Heat the oil in a large pan. Add the pork cubes and cook over a high heat, turning several times until browned all over. Add the onion and garlic and fry gently until soft, then stir in the oregano and chopped jalapeños. Cook for 2 minutes more.

2 Tip the tomatillos into a blender, add the stock and process until smooth. Add to the pork mixture, cover and cook for 30 minutes.

3 Meanwhile, soak the nopalitos (pickled strips of cactus paddles) in cold water for 10 minutes. Drain, then add to the pork mixture and continue cooking for about 10 minutes or until the pork is cooked through and tender.

4 Season the mixture with salt and plenty of ground black pepper to taste. Serve this dish with warm corn tortillas.

Nutritional information per portion: Energy 522kcal/2194kJ; Protein 41g; Carbohydrate 49.5g, of which sugars 4.8g; Fat 18.6g, of which saturates 7g; Cholesterol 106mg; Calcium 251mg; Fibre 3.1g; Sodium 461mg.

Enchiladas with pork and green sauce

The green tomatillo sauce provides a tart contrast to the pork filling in this popular dish.
Cascabels are dried chillies, which rattle when shaken.

SERVES 3–4

500g/1¼ lb pork shoulder, diced
1 cascabel chilli
30ml/2 tbsp oil
2 garlic cloves, crushed
1 onion, finely chopped
300g/11oz/scant 2 cups drained canned
    tomatillos
6 fresh corn tortillas
75g/3oz/¾ cup grated Monterey Jack or
    mild Cheddar cheese

1 Put the diced pork in a pan and pour over water to cover. Bring to the boil, and simmer for 40 minutes. Meanwhile, soak the chilli in hot water for 30 minutes until softened. Drain, remove the stalk, then slit the chilli and scrape out the seeds. Drain the pork, let it cool, and shred. Put in a bowl. Set aside.

2 Heat the oil in a frying pan and fry the garlic and onion for 3–4 minutes until translucent. Chop and add the chilli with the tomatillos. Cook, stirring constantly, until the tomatillos start to break up. Lower the heat and simmer the sauce for 10 minutes more. Cool slightly, then purée in a blender.

3 Preheat the oven to 180°C/350°F/Gas 4. Wrap the tortillas in foil and steam on a plate over boiling water for a few minutes to soften them.

4 Spoon one-sixth of the shredded pork on to the centre of a tortilla and roll it up. Place it in a shallow baking dish that is large enough to hold all the enchiladas in a single layer. Fill and roll the remaining tortillas and add them to the dish. Pour the sauce over and sprinkle with cheese. Bake for 25–30 minutes or until the cheese bubbles. Serve.

Nutritional information per portion: Energy 522kcal/2194kJ; Protein 41g; Carbohydrate 49.5g, of which sugars 4.8g; Fat 18.6g, of which saturates 7g; Cholesterol 106mg; Calcium 251mg; Fibre 3.1g; Sodium 461mg.

Stuffed loin of pork

Pork features twice in this dish, which consists of a roast loin stuffed with minced pork. The perfect centrepiece for a special occasion dinner, it is served at weddings and other celebrations.

SERVES 6

1.5kg/3–3¹/₂ lb boneless pork loin,
   butterflied ready for stuffing

FOR THE STUFFING
50g/2oz/¹/₃ cup raisins
120ml/4fl oz/¹/₂ cup dry white wine
15ml/1 tbsp vegetable oil
1 onion, diced

2 garlic cloves, crushed
2.5ml/¹/₂ tsp ground cloves
5ml/1 tsp ground cinnamon
500g/1¹/₄ lb minced (ground) pork
150ml/¹/₄ pint/²/₃ cup vegetable stock
2 tomatoes
50g/2oz/¹/₂ cup chopped almonds
2.5ml/¹/₂ tsp each salt and black pepper

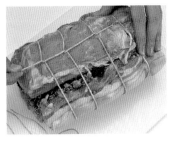

1 Put the raisins and wine in a bowl. Set aside. Heat the oil in a pan, add the onion and garlic and cook for 5 minutes over a low heat. Add the cloves and cinnamon, then the pork. Cook, stirring, until the pork has browned. Add the stock. Simmer, stirring frequently, for 20 minutes.

2 Cut a cross in each tomato base, then put in a heatproof bowl. Pour over boiling water. Leave for 3 minutes, then lift out and plunge into a bowl of cold water. Drain.

3 Remove the tomato skins, then chop the flesh. Stir the tomatoes and almonds into the mince mixture, add the raisins and wine. Cook until reduced to a thick sauce. Leave to cool.

4 Preheat the oven to 180°C/350°F/Gas 4. Open out the pork loin and trim it neatly. Season the stuffing. Spread evenly over the surface of the meat in a neat layer, taking it right to the edges. Roll up the pork loin carefully and tie it at intervals with kitchen string. Weigh the pork and calculate the cooking time at 30 minutes per lb/450g, plus another 30 minutes.

5 Put the stuffed pork joint in a roasting pan, season with salt and pepper and roast until cooked. Transfer to a meat platter, place a tent of foil over it, and let stand for 10 minutes before carving and serving with the roast vegetables of your choice.

Nutritional information per portion: Energy 569kcal/2383kJ; Protein 71.9g; Carbohydrate 11.2g, of which sugars 10.8g; Fat 24.7g, of which saturates 7.1g; Cholesterol 213mg; Calcium 56mg; Fibre 1.3g; Sodium 243mg.

Tortilla pie with chorizo

This is a popular Mexican breakfast dish, known as Chilaquiles. The fried tortilla strips stay crisp in the tomatillo, cream and cheese sauce.

SERVES 6

30ml/2 tbsp vegetable oil
500g/1¼ lb minced (ground) pork
3 garlic cloves, crushed
10ml/2 tsp dried oregano
5ml/1 tsp ground cinnamon
2.5ml/½ tsp ground cloves
2.5ml/½ tsp ground black pepper
30ml/2 tbsp dry sherry
5ml/1 tsp caster (superfine) sugar
5ml/1 tsp salt
12 corn tortillas, freshly made
oil, for frying
350g/12oz/3 cups grated Monterey Jack or mild Cheddar cheese
300ml/½ pint/1¼ cups crème fraîche

FOR THE TOMATILLO SAUCE

300g/11oz/scant 2 cups drained canned tomatillos
60ml/4 tbsp stock or water
2 serrano chillies, seeded and chopped
2 garlic cloves
small bunch of fresh coriander (cilantro)
120ml/4fl oz/½ cup sour cream

1 Preheat the oven to 180°C/350°F/Gas 4. Heat the oil in a large pan. Add the pork and garlic. Stir over a moderate heat until the meat has browned, then stir in the oregano, cinnamon, cloves and pepper. Cook for 3–4 minutes, stirring, then add the sherry, sugar and salt. Stir for 3–4 minutes, then remove the pan from the heat.

2 Cut the tortillas into 2cm/¾ in strips. Pour oil into a frying pan to a depth of 2cm/¾ in and heat to 190°C/375°F. Fry the tortilla strips in batches until crisp and golden brown all over.

3 Spread half the pork mixture in a baking dish. Top with half the tortilla strips and cheese, then add dollops of crème fraîche. Repeat the layers. Bake for 20–25 minutes.

4 To make the sauce, put all the ingredients except the sour cream in a blender. Reserve a little coriander for sprinkling. Process until smooth. Scrape into a pan, bring to the boil, then lower the heat and simmer for 5 minutes.

5 Stir the sour cream into the sauce and season. Pour over the pie and serve, sprinkled with coriander.

Nutritional information per portion: Energy 874kcal/3636kJ; Protein 39.5g; Carbohydrate 40.5g, of which sugars 4.7g; Fat 60.9g, of which saturates 30.5g; Cholesterol 173mg; Calcium 565mg; Fibre 5.4g; Sodium 977mg.

Tostadas with shredded pork and spices

Crisp fried tortillas topped with refried beans and spiced shredded pork make a delectable treat and they are often sold from stalls in Mexican city streets.

SERVES 6

6 corn tortillas, freshly made or a few
   days old
oil, for frying

FOR THE TOPPING

500g/1¼ lb pork shoulder, cut into
   2.5cm/1in cubes
2.5ml/½ tsp salt
15ml/1 tbsp oil
1 small onion, halved and sliced
1 garlic clove, crushed
1 pasilla chilli, seeded and ground
5ml/1 tsp ground cinnamon
2.5ml/½ tsp ground cloves
175g/6oz/1 cup refried beans
90ml/6 tbsp sour cream
2 tomatoes, seeded and diced
115g/4oz feta cheese, crumbled
fresh oregano sprigs, to garnish

1 Make the topping. Place the pork in a pan, pour over water to cover and bring to the boil. Lower the heat, cover and simmer for 40 minutes. Drain. Shred the pork, put it in a bowl and season with the salt.

2 Heat the oil in a large frying pan. Add the onion, garlic, chilli and spices. Stir over the heat for 2–3 minutes, then add the shredded meat and cook until the meat is thoroughly heated and has absorbed the flavourings. Heat the refried beans in a separate, small pan.

3 Meanwhile, cook the tortillas. Pour oil into a frying pan to a depth of 2cm/¾ in. Heat the oil and fry one tortilla at a time, pressing down with a metal spatula to keep it flat. As soon as a tortilla is crisp, lift out and drain on kitchen paper.

4 Place each tortilla on a plate. Top with refried beans. Add a little of the meat, then spoon over 15ml/1 tbsp of the sour cream. Divide the diced tomato among the tostadas and top with the crumbled feta. Serve garnished with fresh oregano.

Nutritional information per portion: Energy 525kcal/2195kJ; Protein 34.8g; Carbohydrate 37.2g, of which sugars 2.9g; Fat 27.3g, of which saturates 5.9g; Cholesterol 92mg; Calcium 104mg; Fibre 3.4g; Sodium 369mg.

Carnitas

Carnitas, literally "little meats", can be eaten as part of a main dish or used to fill tacos or burritos. They are also served with salsa as snacks or antojitos (nibbles).

SERVES 8 AS AN APPETIZER, 6 AS A MAIN COURSE

2 dried bay leaves

10ml/2 tsp dried thyme

5ml/1 tsp dried marjoram

1.5kg/3–3¹/₂ lb mixed boneless pork
  (loin and leg)

3 garlic cloves

2.5ml/¹/₂ tsp salt

200g/7oz/scant 1 cup lard

1 orange, cut into 8 wedges

1 small onion, thickly sliced

warm wheat flour tortillas, to serve

FOR THE SALSA

small bunch of fresh coriander (cilantro)

1 white onion

8–10 pickled jalapeño chilli slices

45ml/3 tbsp freshly squeezed
  orange juice

1 Crumble the bay leaves into a mortar. Add the dried thyme and dried marjoram and grind the mixture with a pestle to a fine powder.

2 Cut the pork into 5cm/2in cubes and place it in a non-metallic bowl. Add the herbs and salt. Using your fingers, rub the spice mixture into the meat. Cover and marinate for at least 2 hours, preferably overnight.

3 To make the salsa, remove the stems from the coriander and chop the leaves roughly. Cut the onion in half, then slice each half thinly. Finely chop the chilli slices. Mix all the salsa ingredients in a bowl, pour over the freshly squeezed orange juice and toss gently to mix. Cover and chill until required.

4 Heat the lard in a flameproof casserole. Add the pork mixture, with the oranges, garlic cloves and onion. Brown the pork cubes on all sides. Using a slotted spoon, lift out the onion and garlic and discard. Cover the casserole and continue to cook over a low heat for about 1¹/₂ hours.

5 Remove the lid and lift out and discard the orange wedges. Continue to cook the mixture, uncovered, until all the meat juices have been absorbed and the pork cubes are crisp on the outside and tender and moist inside. Serve with warm tortillas and the salsa.

Nutritional information per portion: Energy 297kcal/1241kJ; Protein 40.8g; Carbohydrate 2.1g, of which sugars 1.9g; Fat 13.9g, of which saturates 5.1g; Cholesterol 124mg; Calcium 37mg; Fibre 0.7g; Sodium 135mg.

Tamales filled with spiced pork

These tamales are among the most ancient of Mexican foods. At one time the neat little corn husk parcels filled with plain, savoury or sweet masa dough were cooked in the ashes of a wood fire. Today they are more likely to be steamed, but the thrill of unwrapping them remains the same.

SERVES 6

500g/1¼lb lean pork, cut into 5cm/2in cubes
750ml/1¼ pints/3 cups chicken stock
600g/1lb 6oz/4½ cups *masa harina*
450g/1lb/2 cups lard or white cooking fat, softened
30ml/2 tbsp salt
12 large or 24 small dried corn husks

2 ancho chillies, seeded
15ml/1 tbsp vegetable oil
½ onion, finely chopped
2–3 garlic cloves, crushed
2.5ml/½ tsp allspice berries
2 dried bay leaves
2.5ml/½ tsp ground cumin
lime wedges, to serve (optional)

1 Put the pork cubes in a large pan. Pour over water to cover. Bring to the boil, lower the heat and simmer for 40 minutes.

2 Meanwhile, heat the chicken stock in a separate pan. Put the *masa harina* in a large bowl and add the hot stock, a little at a time, to make a stiff dough.

3 Put the lard in another bowl and beat with an electric whisk until light and fluffy, as when beating butter for a cake. Test by dropping a small amount of the whipped lard into a cup of water. If it floats, it is ready for use.

4 Continue to beat the lard, gradually adding the *masa* dough. When the mixture is spreadable, beat in the salt. Cover with clear film (plastic wrap) to prevent the mixture from drying out.

5 Put the corn husks in a bowl and pour over boiling water to cover. Leave to soak for 30 minutes. Soak the seeded chillies in a separate bowl of hot water for the same time.

6 Drain the pork, reserving 105ml/7 tbsp of the liquid, and chop the meat finely. Heat the oil in a pan and fry the onion and garlic over a moderate heat for 2–3 minutes. Drain the chillies, chop finely and add to the pan. Put the allspice and bay leaves in a mortar, grind with a pestle, then work in the ground cumin. Add to the onion mixture and stir well. Cook for 2–3 minutes. Add the pork and reserved cooking liquid and continue cooking until the liquid is absorbed. Leave to cool.

7 Drain the corn husks and pat them dry in a clean dishtowel. Place one large corn husk on a board. Spoon one-twelfth of the masa mixture on to the centre of the husk and spread almost to the sides.

8 Place a spoonful of the meat mixture on top of the *masa*. Fold the two long sides of the corn husk over the filling, then bring up each of the two shorter sides in turn, to make a neat parcel. Slide one of the two short sides inside the other, if possible, to prevent the parcel from unravelling, or tie with string or strips of the corn husk.

9 Place the *tamales* in a steamer basket over a pan of steadily simmering water and steam for about 1 hour, topping up the water as needed. To test if the *tamales* are ready, unwrap one. The filling should peel away from the husk cleanly. Pile the *tamales*, still sealed, on a serving plate. Leave to stand for about 10 minutes, then serve with lime wedges, if liked.

Nutritional information per portion: Energy 848kcal/3528kJ; Protein 38.1g; Carbohydrate 74g, of which sugars 0.6g; Fat 43.5g, of which saturates 15.5g; Cholesterol 114mg; Calcium 18mg; Fibre 2.3g; Sodium 94mg.

Lamb stew with chilli sauce

The chillies in this stew add depth and richness to the sauce, while the potato slices ensure that it is substantial enough to serve on its own.

SERVES 6

6 guajillo chillies, seeded
2 pasilla chillies, seeded
250ml/8fl oz/1 cup hot water
3 garlic cloves, peeled
5ml/1 tsp ground cinnamon
2.5ml/¹⁄₂ tsp ground cloves
2.5ml/¹⁄₂ tsp ground black pepper
15ml/1 tbsp vegetable oil
1kg/2¹⁄₄lb lean boneless lamb shoulder,
    cut into 2cm/³⁄₄in cubes
400g/14oz potatoes, scrubbed and cut
    into 1cm/¹⁄₂in thick slices
salt
strips of red (bell) pepper and fresh
    oregano, to garnish

1 Snap or tear the dried chillies into large pieces, put them in a bowl and pour over the hot water. Leave to soak for 30 minutes, then tip the contents of the bowl into a food processor or blender. Add the garlic and spices. Process until smooth.

2 Heat the oil in a large pan. Add the lamb cubes, in batches, and stir-fry over a high heat until the cubes are browned on all sides.

3 Return all the lamb cubes to the pan, spread them out, then cover them with a layer of potato slices. Add salt to taste. Put a lid on the pan and cook over a medium heat for 10 minutes.

4 Pour over the chilli mixture and mix well. Replace the lid and simmer over a low heat for about 1 hour or until the meat and the potato are tender. Serve with a rice dish, and garnish with strips of red pepper and oregano.

Nutritional information per portion: Energy 370kcal/1547kJ; Protein 34.8g; Carbohydrate 10.8g, of which sugars 0.9g; Fat 21.2g, of which saturates 9.1g; Cholesterol 129mg; Calcium 21mg; Fibre 0.7g; Sodium 154mg.

Beef enchiladas with red sauce

Enchiladas are usually made with corn tortillas, although in parts of northern Mexico flour tortillas are sometimes used.

SERVES 3–4

500g/1¼ lb rump (round) steak, cut into
    5cm/2in cubes
2 ancho chillies, seeded
2 pasilla chillies, seeded
2 garlic cloves, crushed
10ml/2 tsp dried oregano
2.5ml/½ tsp ground cumin
30ml/2 tbsp vegetable oil
7 fresh corn tortillas
shredded onion and flat-leaf parsley,
    to garnish
salsa, to serve

1 Put the steak in a deep frying pan and cover with water. Bring to the boil, then lower the heat and simmer for 1–1½ hours, or until very tender.

2 Meanwhile, put the dried chillies in a bowl and pour over the hot water. Leave to soak for 30 minutes, then tip the contents of the bowl into a blender and whizz to a smooth paste.

3 Drain the steak and let it cool, reserving 250ml/8fl oz/1 cup of the cooking liquid. Fry the garlic, oregano and cumin in the oil for 2 minutes. Stir in the chilli paste and the reserved cooking liquid. Tear one of the tortillas into small pieces and add it to the mixture. Bring to the boil, then lower the heat. Simmer for 10 minutes, stirring occasionally, until thickened. Shred the steak and stir it into the sauce, then heat through for a few minutes.

4 Wrap the tortillas and steam on a plate over boiling water until pliable. Divide the meat mixture between the tortillas and roll them up to make enchiladas. Garnish with shreds of onion and parsley and serve with the salsa.

Nutritional information per portion: Energy 460kcal/1939kJ; Protein 38g; Carbohydrate 52.4g, of which sugars 1.1g; Fat 12.3g, of which saturates 3.1g; Cholesterol 84mg; Calcium 108mg; Fibre 2.1g; Sodium 331mg.

Tacos with shredded beef

In Mexico tacos are most often made with soft corn tortillas, which are filled and folded in half. It is unusual to see the crisp shells of corn that are so widely used in Tex-Mex cooking.

SERVES 6

450g/1lb rump (round) steak, diced
150g/5oz/1 cup *masa harina*
2.5ml/1/2 tsp salt
120ml/4fl oz/1/2 cup warm water
10ml/2 tsp dried oregano
5ml/1 tsp ground cumin
30ml/2 tbsp oil
1 onion, thinly sliced
2 garlic cloves, crushed
fresh coriander (cilantro), to garnish
shredded lettuce, lime wedges and Classic
    Tomato Salsa, to serve

1 Put the steak in a deep frying pan and pour over water to cover. Bring to the boil, then lower the heat and simmer for 1–1½ hours.

2 Mix the *masa harina* and salt in a bowl. Add the water gradually to make a dough. Knead the dough on a lightly floured surface for 3–4 minutes until smooth, then wrap it in clear film (plastic wrap) and leave to rest for 1 hour.

3 Let the cooked meat cool slightly, then shred it. Put the meat in a bowl. Divide the dough into six balls. Open a tortilla press and line both sides with plastic. Put each ball on the press and flatten it into a 15–20cm/6–8in round.

4 Heat a griddle or frying pan until hot. Cook each tortilla for 15–20 seconds on each side, and then for a further 15 seconds on the first side.

5 Add the oregano and cumin to the meat and mix well. Heat the oil in a pan and fry the onion and garlic for 3–4 minutes until softened. Add the meat and toss over the heat until heated through. Place some lettuce on a tortilla, top with the beef and salsa, fold in half and serve with lime wedges and coriander.

Nutritional information per portion: Energy 202kcal/846kJ; Protein 18.8g; Carbohydrate 14.9g, of which sugars 0.5g; Fat 7.4g, of which saturates 1.7g; Cholesterol 44mg; Calcium 6mg; Fibre 0.7g; Sodium 46mg.

Albondigas

Don't be daunted by the length of the ingredient list. These meatballs are absolutely delicious and the chipotle chilli gives the sauce a distinctive, slightly smoky flavour.

SERVES 4

225g/8oz minced (ground) pork
225g/8oz lean minced (ground) beef
1 onion, finely chopped
50g/2oz/1 cup fresh white breadcrumbs
5ml/1 tsp dried oregano
2.5ml/¹/₂ tsp ground cumin
2.5ml/¹/₂ tsp salt
2.5ml/¹/₂ tsp ground black pepper
1 egg, beaten
oil, for frying
fresh oregano sprigs, to garnish

FOR THE SAUCE

1 chipotle chilli, seeded
15ml/1 tbsp vegetable oil
1 onion, finely chopped
2 garlic cloves, crushed
175ml/6fl oz/³/₄ cup beef stock
400g/14oz can chopped tomatoes in
    tomato juice
105ml/7 tbsp passata

1 Mix the pork and beef in a bowl. Add the onion, breadcrumbs, oregano, cumin, salt and pepper and mix until well combined. Stir in the egg, mix well, then roll into 4cm/1¹/₂ in balls. Put these on a baking sheet and chill.

2 Soak the dried chilli in hot water to cover for 15 minutes. Heat the oil in a pan and fry the onion and garlic for 3–4 minutes until softened.

3 Drain the chilli, reserving the soaking water, then chop it and add it to the onion mixture. Fry for 1 minute, then stir in the beef stock, tomatoes, passata and soaking water, with salt and pepper to taste. Bring to the boil, lower the heat and simmer, stirring occasionally, while you cook the meatballs.

4 Heat the oil for frying in a frying pan and fry the meatballs in batches for about 5 minutes, turning them occasionally, until browned.

5 Drain off the oil and transfer all the meatballs to a shallow casserole. Pour over the sauce and simmer for 10 minutes, stirring gently from time to time. Garnish with the oregano and serve.

Nutritional information per portion: Energy 420kcal/1759kJ; Protein 29g; Carbohydrate 33.5g, of which sugars 10.3g; Fat 19.9g, of which saturates 6.8g; Cholesterol 119mg; Calcium 88mg; Fibre 3.2g; Sodium 322mg.

Stuffed beef with cheese and chilli sauce

This recipe had its origins in northern Mexico or in New Mexico, which is beef country. It is a good way to cook steaks, either under the grill or on the barbecue.

SERVES 4

4 fresh serrano chillies
115g/4oz/1/2 cup full-fat soft cheese
30ml/2 tbsp reposada tequila
30ml/2 tbsp oil
1 onion
2 garlic cloves
5ml/1 tsp dried oregano

2.5ml/1/2 tsp salt
2.5ml/1/2 tsp ground black pepper
175g/6oz/11/2 cups grated medium
    Cheddar cheese
4 fillet steaks (beef tenderloin), at least
    2.5cm/1in thick

1 Dry roast the chillies in a griddle pan over a moderate heat, turning them frequently until the skins are blistered but not burnt. Put them in a strong plastic bag and tie the top to keep the steam in. Set aside for 20 minutes.

2 Remove the chillies from the bag, slit them and scrape out the seeds with a knife. Cut the flesh into strips, then cut each strip into several shorter strips.

3 Put the full-fat soft cheese in a small heavy pan and stir over a low heat until it has melted. Add the chilli strips and the tequila and stir to make a smooth sauce. Keep warm over a very low heat.

4 Heat the oil in a frying pan and fry the onion, garlic and oregano for about 5 minutes over a moderate heat, stirring frequently until the onion has browned. Season with the salt and pepper.

5 Remove the frying pan from the heat and stir the grated cheese into the onion mixture.

6 Cut each steak almost but not quite in half across its width, so that it can be opened out, butterfly-fashion. Preheat the grill to its highest setting.

7 Spoon a quarter of the cheese and onion filling on to one side of each steak and close the other side over it. Place the steaks in a grill (broiler) pan and grill (broil) for 3–5 minutes on each side, depending on how you like your steak. Serve on heated plates with the vegetables of your choice, and with the cheese and chilli sauce poured over.

Nutritional information per portion: Energy 640kcal/2659kJ; Protein 56.1g; Carbohydrate 1.3g, of which sugars 1g; Fat 44.8g, of which saturates 23.5g; Cholesterol 201mg; Calcium 329mg; Fibre 0.2g; Sodium 508mg.

Vegetable and brunch dishes

When the Spaniards arrived in Mexico they

discovered that the indigenous people

cultivated a wide range of vegetables,

such as corn, bell peppers and green beans,

that Europeans were then unfamiliar

with. The range of recipes in this chapter is

testimony to the variety of vegetables that

is still being eaten in Mexico today.

Potatoes with chorizo and green chillies

This recipe makes a delicious brunch dish. Typical of peasant food, it is based on the combination of plenty of potato mixed with strongly flavoured meat to help it go further.

SERVES 4–6

900g/2lb potatoes, peeled and diced
30ml/2 tbsp vegetable oil
2 garlic cloves, crushed
4 spring onions (scallions), chopped
2 fresh jalapeño chillies, seeded and diced
300g/11oz chorizo sausage, skinned
150g/5oz/1¼ cups grated Monterey Jack
   or Cheddar cheese
salt (optional)

1 Bring a large pan of water to the boil and add the potatoes. When the water returns to the boil, lower the heat and simmer the potatoes for 5 minutes. Tip the potatoes into a colander and drain thoroughly.

2 Heat the oil in a large frying pan, add the garlic, spring onions and chillies and cook for 3–4 minutes. Add the diced potato and cook until the cubes begin to brown a little.

3 Cut the chorizo into small cubes and add these to the pan. Cook the mixture for 5 minutes more, until the sausage has heated through.

4 Season with salt if necessary, then add the cheese. Mix quickly and carefully, trying not to break up the cubes of potato. Serve immediately, while the cheese is still melting.

Nutritional information per portion: Energy 443kcal/1847kJ; Protein 16g; Carbohydrate 32.4g, of which sugars 3.6g; Fat 28.1g, of which saturates 12.3g; Cholesterol 49mg; Calcium 226mg; Fibre 1.9g; Sodium 728mg.

Potato cakes

Quick and easy to make, these potato cakes are very moreish. Serve them with salsa as a light meal, or as an accompaniment to roast or pan-fried meats.

MAKES 10

600g/1lb 6oz potatoes, peeled and
    halved
115g/4oz/1 cup grated Cheddar cheese
2.5ml/1/2 tsp salt
50g/2oz/1/3 cup drained pickled jalapeño
    chilli slices, finely chopped (optional)
1 egg, beaten
small bunch of fresh coriander (cilantro),
    finely chopped
plain (all-purpose) flour, for shaping
oil, for shallow frying
salsa, to serve

1 Add the potatoes to a pan of cold water. Bring to the boil and cook for about 30 minutes, until tender. Drain, return to the pan and mash.

2 Scrape the potato into a bowl and stir in the grated cheese, with the salt and the chopped jalapeños, if using. Stir in the beaten egg and most of the chopped coriander and mix to a dough.

3 When the dough is cool enough to handle, put it on a board. With floured hands, divide it into ten balls, then flatten each ball to a cake.

4 Heat the oil in a large frying pan. Fry the potato cakes, in batches if necessary, for 2–3 minutes over a moderate heat. Turn them over and cook until both sides are golden. Pile on a platter, sprinkle with salt and the remaining chopped coriander and serve with salsa.

Nutritional information per portion: Energy 137kcal/573kJ; Protein 4.8g; Carbohydrate 12.2g, of which sugars 1.1g; Fat 7.7g, of which saturates 3g; Cholesterol 30mg; Calcium 99mg; Fibre 1g; Sodium 96mg.

Red cauliflower

Vegetables are seldom served plain in Mexico. The cauliflower here is flavoured with a simple tomato salsa and fresh cheese. The salsa could be any table salsa; tomatillo is particularly good.

SERVES 6

1 small onion, very finely chopped
1 lime
1 medium cauliflower, cut into florets
400g/14oz can chopped tomatoes
4 fresh serrano chillies, seeded and
    finely chopped
1.5ml/¼ tsp caster (superfine) sugar
75g/3oz feta cheese, crumbled
salt
chopped fresh flat leaf parsley,
    to garnish

1 Place the onion in a bowl. Peel away the zest of the lime in thin strips. Add to the chopped onion.

2 Cut the lime in half and add the juice from both halves to the onions and lime zest mixture.

3 Tip the tomatoes into a pan and add the chillies and sugar. Heat gently. Meanwhile, place the cauliflower in a pan of boiling water and cook gently until tender.

4 Add the onions to the tomato salsa, with salt to taste, stir in and heat through, then spoon about a third of the salsa into a serving dish.

5 Drain the cauliflower and arrange the florets on top of the salsa, then spoon the remaining salsa on top.

6 Sprinkle with the feta, which should soften a little on contact. Serve immediately, sprinkled with chopped fresh flat leaf parsley.

Nutritional information per portion: Energy 81kcal/338kJ; Protein 5.9g; Carbohydrate 5.6g, of which sugars 4.9g; Fat 4g, of which saturates 2.3g; Cholesterol 11mg; Calcium 79mg; Fibre 2.3g; Sodium 230mg.

Pumpkin with spices

Roasted pumpkin has a wonderful, rich flavour. Eat it straight from the skin, eat the skin too, or scoop out the cooked flesh, add a spoonful of salsa and wrap it in a warm tortilla. It also makes flavoursome soups and sauces.

SERVES 6

1kg/2¼ lb pumpkin
50g/2oz/¼ cup butter, melted
10ml/2 tsp hot chilli sauce
2.5ml/½ tsp salt
2.5ml/½ tsp ground allspice
5ml/1 tsp ground cinnamon
chopped fresh herbs, to garnish
Classic Tomato Salsa and crème fraîche,
    to serve

1 Preheat the oven to 220°C/ 425°F/Gas 7. Cut the pumpkin into large pieces. Scoop out and discard the fibre and seeds, then put the pumpkin pieces in a roasting pan.

2 Mix the melted butter and chilli sauce and drizzle the mixture evenly over the pumpkin pieces.

3 Put the salt in a bowl and add the allspice and cinnamon. Sprinkle the mixture over the pumpkin.

4 Roast for 25 minutes or until the pumpkin flesh yields when pressed gently. Serve on a heated platter and offer the tomato salsa and crème fraîche separately.

Nutritional information per portion: Energy 68kcal/284kJ; Protein 1.8g; Carbohydrate 5.4g, of which sugars 2.9g; Fat 4.5g, of which saturates 2.3g; Cholesterol 9mg; Calcium 92mg; Fibre 3.2g; Sodium 55mg.

Stuffed chillies in a walnut sauce

The potato and meat filling in these chillies is a good partner for the rich, creamy walnut sauce that covers them.

SERVES 4

8 ancho chillies

1 large potato, about 200g/7oz

45ml/3 tbsp vegetable oil

115g/4oz lean minced (ground) pork

1 onion, chopped

5ml/1 tsp ground cinnamon

115g/4oz/1 cup walnuts, chopped

50g/2oz/1/2 cup chopped almonds

150g/5oz/2/3 cup cream cheese

50g/2oz/1/2 cup soft goat's cheese

120ml/4fl oz/1/2 cup single (light) cream

120ml/4fl oz/1/2 cup dry sherry

50g/2oz/1/2 cup plain (all-purpose) flour

2.5ml/1/2 tsp ground white pepper

2 eggs, separated

oil, for deep frying

salt

chopped fresh herbs, to garnish

1 Soak the dried chillies in a bowl of hot water for 30 minutes until softened. Drain, cut off the stalks, then slit them down one side. Scrape out the seeds with a small sharp knife, taking care to keep the chillies intact for stuffing.

2 Peel the potato and cut it into 1cm/1/2 in cubes. Heat 15ml/1 tbsp of the oil in a large frying pan, add the pork mince and cook, stirring, until it has browned evenly.

3 Add the potato cubes and mix well. Cover and cook over a low heat for 25–30 minutes, stirring occasionally. Do not worry if the potato sticks to the bottom of the pan. Season with salt, remove from the heat and set aside.

4 Heat the remaining oil in a separate frying pan and fry the onion with the cinnamon for 3–4 minutes or until softened. Stir in the nuts and fry for 3–4 minutes more.

5 Add both types of cheese to the pan, with the cream and sherry. Mix well. Reduce the heat to the lowest setting and cook until the cheese melts and the sauce starts to thicken. Taste and season with salt if necessary.

6 Spread out the flour on a plate or in a shallow dish. Season with the white pepper. Beat the egg yolks in a bowl until they are pale and thick.

7 In a separate, grease-free bowl, whisk the whites until they form soft peaks. Add a generous pinch of salt, then fold in the yolks, a little at a time.

8 Spoon some of the filling into each chilli. Pat the outside dry with kitchen paper. Heat the oil for deep frying to a temperature of 180°C/350°F.

9 Coat a chilli in flour, then dip it in the egg batter, covering it completely. Drain for a few seconds, then add to the hot oil. Add several more battered chillies, but do not overcrowd the pan. Fry the chillies until golden, then drain on kitchen paper and keep hot while cooking successive batches.

10 Reheat the sauce over a low heat, if necessary. Arrange the chillies on individual plates, spoon a little sauce over each and serve immediately, sprinkled with chopped fresh herbs. A green salad goes well with this dish.

Nutritional information per portion: Energy 989kcal/4098kJ; Protein 29.2g; Carbohydrate 27.3g, of which sugars 4.7g; Fat 84g, of which saturates 28g; Cholesterol 202mg; Calcium 238mg; Fibre 3.2g; Sodium 415mg.

Mexican-style green peas

This is a great way of cooking fresh peas, and makes a perfect accompaniment to any meal.

SERVES 4

2 tomatoes
50g/2oz/¼ cup butter
2 garlic cloves, halved
1 medium onion, halved and thinly sliced
400g/14oz/scant 3 cups shelled fresh peas
30ml/2 tbsp water
salt and ground black pepper
fresh chives, to garnish

1 Cut a cross in each tomato base. Place the tomatoes in a heatproof bowl and pour over boiling water to cover. Leave for 3 minutes, then plunge into a bowl of cold water. Drain. Remove the skins. Cut in half and squeeze out the seeds. Chop the flesh into 1cm/½ in dice.

2 Melt the butter in a pan. Cook the garlic until golden, then lift out on a slotted spoon and discard. Add the onion slices to the pan and fry until transparent.

3 Add the tomato to the onion, mix well, then stir in the peas. Pour over the water, lower the heat and cover the pan tightly. Cook for 10 minutes, shaking the pan occasionally to stop the mixture from sticking.

4 Check that the peas are cooked, then season with plenty of salt and pepper. Transfer the mixture to a heated dish and serve, garnished with fresh chives.

Nutritional information per portion: Energy 232kcal/958kJ; Protein 11g; Carbohydrate 19.8g, of which sugars 5.9g; Fat 12.7g, of which saturates 7g; Cholesterol 27mg; Calcium 41mg; Fibre 7.8g; Sodium 82mg.

Mushrooms with chipotle chillies

The smoky flavour of chipotle chillies is the perfect foil for the mushrooms in this salad.

SERVES 6

2 chipotle chillies
450g/1lb/6 cups button (white) mushrooms
60ml/4 tbsp vegetable oil
1 onion, finely chopped
2 garlic cloves, crushed or chopped
salt
small bunch of fresh coriander (cilantro),
    to garnish

1 Soak the dried chillies in a bowl of hot water for about 10 minutes until they are softened. Drain, cut off the stalks, then slit the chillies and scrape out the seeds. Chop the flesh finely.

2 Trim the mushrooms, then clean them with a damp cloth or kitchen paper. If they are large, cut them in half.

3 Heat the oil in a large frying pan. Add the onion, garlic, chillies and mushrooms and stir until evenly coated in the oil. Fry for 6–8 minutes, stirring occasionally, until the onion and mushrooms are tender.

4 Season to taste and spoon into a serving dish. Chop some of the coriander, leaving some whole leaves, and use to garnish. Serve hot.

Nutritional information per portion: Energy 69kcal/287kJ; Protein 2.4g; Carbohydrate 1.3g, of which sugars 0.9g; Fat 6.1g, of which saturates 0.8g; Cholesterol 0mg; Calcium 14mg; Fibre 1.2g; Sodium 7mg.

Courgettes with cheese and green chillies

This is a very tasty way to serve courgettes, often a rather bland vegetable, and the dish looks good too. Serve it as a vegetarian main dish or an unusual side dish.

SERVES 6 AS AN ACCOMPANIMENT

30ml/2 tbsp vegetable oil
1/2 onion, thinly sliced
2 garlic cloves, crushed
5ml/1 tsp dried oregano
2 tomatoes
50g/2oz/1/3 cup drained pickled jalapeño chilli slices, chopped
500g/11/4 lb courgettes (zucchini)
115g/4oz/1/2 cup cream cheese
salt and ground black pepper
fresh oregano sprigs, to garnish

1 Heat the oil in a frying pan. Add the onion, garlic and dried oregano. Fry for 3–4 minutes, until the onion is soft and translucent.

2 Cut a cross in the base of each tomato. Place in a heatproof bowl and cover with boiling water. Leave in the water for 3 minutes, then lift out on a slotted spoon and plunge into a bowl of cold water. Drain. The skins will have begun to peel back from the crosses. Remove the skins and cut the tomatoes in half and squeeze out the seeds. Chop the flesh into strips.

3 Top and tail the courgettes, then cut them lengthways into 1cm/1/2 in wide strips. Slice the strips into matchsticks.

4 Stir the courgettes into the onion mixture and fry for 10 minutes, stirring occasionally, until just tender. Add the tomatoes and chopped jalapeños and cook for 2–3 minutes more.

5 Add the cream cheese. Reduce the heat to the lowest setting. As the cheese melts, stir gently to coat the courgettes. Season with salt, pile into a heated dish and serve, garnished with fresh oregano.

Nutritional information per portion: Energy 167kcal/687kJ; Protein 3g; Carbohydrate 2.7g, of which sugars 2.6g; Fat 16.1g, of which saturates 8g; Cholesterol 24mg; Calcium 53mg; Fibre 1.1g; Sodium 80mg.

Courgette torte

This dish looks rather like a Spanish omelette, which is traditionally served at room temperature. Serve warm or prepare it in advance and leave to cool, but do not refrigerate.

SERVES 4–6

500g/1¼ lb courgettes (zucchini)
60ml/4 tbsp vegetable oil
1 small onion
3 fresh jalapeño chillies, seeded and
    cut in strips
3 large eggs
50g/2oz/½ cup self-raising (self-rising)
    flour
115g/4oz/1 cup grated Monterey Jack
    or mild Cheddar cheese
2.5ml/½ tsp cayenne pepper
15g/½ oz/1 tbsp butter
salt

1 Preheat the oven to 180°C/350°F/Gas 4. Top and tail the courgettes, then slice them thinly. Heat the oil in a large frying pan. Add the courgettes and cook for a few minutes, turning them over at least once, until they are soft and beginning to brown. Using a slotted spoon, transfer them to a bowl.

2 Slice the onion and add it to the oil remaining in the pan, with most of the jalapeño strips, reserving some for the garnish. Fry until the onions has softened and are golden. Using a slotted spoon, add the onions and jalapeños to the courgettes.

3 Beat the eggs in a large bowl. Add the self-raising flour, cheese and cayenne. Mix well, then stir in the courgette mixture, with salt to taste.

4 Grease a 23cm/9in round shallow ovenproof dish with the butter. Pour in the courgette mixture and bake for 30 minutes until risen, firm to the touch and golden. Allow to cool.

5 Serve the courgette torte in wedges, garnished with the remaining jalapeño strips. A tomato salad with chives makes a colourful accompaniment.

Nutritional information per portion: Energy 252kcal/1050kJ; Protein 10.9g; Carbohydrate 15.4g, of which sugars 2.7g; Fat 16.4g, of which saturates 6.5g; Cholesterol 117mg; Calcium 226mg; Fibre 1.6g; Sodium 232mg.

Refried beans

These are not actually fried twice, but they are cooked twice, first as Frijoles de Olla and then by frying in fat. These are much better than canned refried beans, which can be rather bland.

SERVES 4

25g/1oz/2 tbsp lard or white cooking fat

2 onions, finely chopped

5ml/1 tsp ground cumin

5ml/1 tsp ground coriander

1 quantity Frijoles de Olla, without the toppings

3 garlic cloves, crushed

small bunch of fresh coriander (cilantro) or 4–5 dried avocado leaves

50g/2oz feta cheese

salt

1 Melt the lard or fat in a frying pan. Add the onions, cumin and ground coriander. Cook gently over a low heat for about 30 minutes or until the onions caramelize and become soft.

2 Add a ladleful of the soft, cooked beans. Fry them for a few minutes to heat. Mash the beans into the onions as they cook, using a fork or a potato masher. Gradually add the beans, then stir in the crushed garlic.

3 Lower the heat and cook the beans to form a thick paste. Season with salt and spoon the mixture into a warmed serving dish.

4 Strip the leaves from the fresh coriander and chop them, or crumble the avocado leaves, and sprinkle most of them over the beans. Crumble the feta cheese over the top, then garnish with the reserved sprigs or leaves.

Nutritional information per portion: Energy 279kcal/1174kJ; Protein 16.9g; Carbohydrate 32.8g, of which sugars 5.4g; Fat 9.9g, of which saturates 4.4g; Cholesterol 15mg; Calcium 148mg; Fibre 11.3g; Sodium 197mg.

Frijoles de olla

Travellers often say that "beans in a pot", as it is translated, taste different in Mexico from those cooked anywhere else. Traditionally, clay pots are used, which gives a slightly earthy flavour.

SERVES 4

250g/9oz/1¼ cups dried pinto beans,
   soaked overnight in water to cover
1.75 litres/3 pints/7½ cups water
2 onions, halved
10 garlic cloves, peeled and left whole
small bunch of fresh coriander (cilantro),
   chopped, plus extra leaves to garnish
salt

FOR THE TOPPINGS
2 fresh red fresno chillies
1 tomato, peeled and chopped
2 spring onions (scallions), finely chopped
60ml/4 tbsp sour cream
50g/2oz feta cheese

1 Drain the beans, rinse and drain again. Put the water in a pan, bring to the boil and add the beans.

2 Add the onions and garlic to the pan. Bring to the boil again, then lower the heat and simmer for 1½ hours, until the beans are tender and there is only a little liquid remaining.

3 Meanwhile, prepare the toppings. Dry fry the chillies in a griddle pan until scorched. Put in a plastic bag and tie the top. Set aside for 20 minutes then remove from the bag.

4 Peel off the chilli skins. Cut off the stalks, then slit the chillies and scrape out the seeds. Cut the flesh into strips and put it in a bowl. Spoon the other toppings into bowls.

5 Ladle about 250ml/8fl oz/1 cup of the beans and liquid into a blender. Process until smooth.

6 Return the bean purée to the pan, add the chopped coriander, season with salt and mix well. Ladle the beans into bowls, add coriander to garnish and serve with the toppings.

Nutritional information per portion: Energy 255kcal/1074kJ; Protein 17.9g; Carbohydrate 32.7g, of which sugars 4.4g; Fat 6.7g, of which saturates 3.8g; Cholesterol 18mg; Calcium 154mg; Fibre 11.4g; Sodium 205mg.

Frijoles charros

These "cowboy beans" taste rather like Boston baked beans, but with rather more punch.
The flavour improves on keeping, so make the beans the day before you intend to serve them.

SERVES 6

2 x 400g/14oz cans pinto beans
120ml/4fl oz/1/2 cup Mexican beer
115g/4oz/2/3 cups drained pickled
   jalapeño chilli slices
2 tomatoes, peeled and chopped
5ml/1 tsp ground cinnamon
175g/6oz bacon fat
1 onion, chopped
2 garlic cloves, crushed
175g/6oz rindless smoked lean bacon,
   diced
45ml/3 tbsp soft dark brown sugar
wheat flour tortillas, to serve

1 Put the drained pinto beans in a pan. Stir in the beer and cook over a high heat for 5 minutes, until some of the beer has been absorbed.

2 Lower the heat slightly and stir in the chillies, then add the tomatoes and cinnamon. Continue to cook, stirring occasionally, for about 10 minutes.

3 Meanwhile, heat the bacon fat in a frying pan until the fat runs. Discard the bacon, then add the onion and garlic to the pan and fry for about 5 minutes, until browned. Transfer the garlic and onions to the beans and mix well.

4 Add the diced smoked bacon to the fat remaining in the frying pan and fry until crisp. Add the bacon and any remaining fat to the beans and mix well.

5 Stir in the sugar. Cook the bean and bacon mixture over a low heat, stirring constantly, until the sugar is dissolved. Serve immediately or spoon into a bowl, leave to cool, cover, then chill for reheating next day. Serve with warmed wheat flour tortillas.

Nutritional information per portion: Energy 454kcal/1890kJ; Protein 13.9g; Carbohydrate 32.7g, of which sugars 13.7g; Fat 29.8g, of which saturates 11.8g; Cholesterol 37mg; Calcium 106mg; Fibre 8.6g; Sodium 911mg.

Corn with cream

In Mexico, this would be made with "heavy cream", the American equivalent of double cream, but the sauce has a better consistency when made with full-fat soft cheese.

SERVES 6 AS A SIDE DISH

4 corn cobs
50g/2oz/¹/₄ cup butter
1 small onion, finely chopped
115g/4oz/²/₃ cup drained pickled
   jalapeño chilli slices
130g/4¹/₂ oz/²/₃ cup full-fat soft cheese
25g/1oz/¹/₃ cup freshly grated Parmesan
   cheese, plus shavings, to garnish
salt and ground black pepper

1 Strip off the husks from the corn and pull off the silks. Place the cobs in a bowl of water and use a vegetable brush to remove any remaining silks. Stand each cob in turn on a board and slice off the kernels, cutting as close to the cob as possible.

2 Melt the butter in a pan, add the chopped onion and fry for 4–5 minutes, stirring occasionally, until the onion has softened and is translucent.

3 Add the corn kernels and cook for 4–5 minutes, until they are just tender. Chop the jalapeños finely and stir them into the corn mixture.

4 Stir in the soft cheese and the grated Parmesan. Cook over a low heat until both cheeses have melted and the corn kernels are coated in the mixture. Season to taste, tip into a heated dish and serve, topped with Parmesan.

Nutritional information per portion: Energy 328kcal/1367kJ; Protein 7.6g; Carbohydrate 27.7g, of which sugars 10.4g; Fat 21.6g, of which saturates 12.8g; Cholesterol 45mg; Calcium 126mg; Fibre 1.5g; Sodium 463mg.

Green butter beans in a **sauce**

Makes the most of butter beans or broad beans by teaming them with tomatoes and fresh chillies for a slightly piquant taste.

SERVES 4

450g/1lb fresh butter (lima) beans or broad (fava) beans
30ml/2 tbsp olive oil
1 onion, finely chopped
2 garlic cloves, crushed
400g/14oz can plum tomatoes, drained and chopped
25g/1oz/about 3 tbsp drained pickled jalapeño
    chilli slices, chopped
salt
fresh coriander (cilantro) and lemon slices, to garnish

1 Bring a pan of lightly salted water to the boil. Add the lima beans or broad beans and cook for 15 minutes, or until just tender.

2 Heat the oil in a frying pan, add the onion and garlic and sauté until the onion is translucent. Tip in the tomatoes and continue to cook, stirring, until thickened.

3 Add the chilli slices and cook for 1–2 minutes. Season with salt to taste.

4 Drain the beans and return them to the pan. Pour over the tomato mixture and stir over the heat for a few minutes. If the sauce thickens too quickly add a little water. Spoon into a serving dish, garnish with the coriander and lemon slices and serve.

Nutritional information per portion: Energy 168kcal/707kJ; Protein 10.5g; Carbohydrate 17.6g, of which sugars 5.6g; Fat 6.7g, of which saturates 1g; Cholesterol 0mg; Calcium 81mg; Fibre 8.5g; Sodium 20mg.

Green beans with **eggs**

This is an unusual way of cooking runner beans, but tastes delicious. Try this for a light supper or as an accompaniment to a roast.

SERVES 6

300g/11oz runner (green) beans, topped, tailed and halved
30ml/2 tbsp vegetable oil
1 onion, halved and thinly sliced
3 eggs
salt and ground black pepper
50g/2oz/¹⁄₂ cup grated Monterey Jack or mild Cheddar cheese
strips of lemon rind, to garnish

1 Bring a pan of water to the boil, add the beans and cook for 5–6 minutes or until tender. Drain in a colander, rinse under cold water to preserve the bright colour, then drain the beans once more.

2 Heat the oil in a frying pan and fry the onion slices for 3–4 minutes until soft and translucent. Break the eggs into a bowl and beat them with seasoning.

3 Add the egg mixture to the onion. Cook slowly over a moderate heat, stirring constantly so that the egg is lightly scrambled. The egg should be moist throughout. Do not overcook.

4 Add the beans to the pan and cook for a few minutes until warmed through. Tip the mixture into a heated serving dish, sprinkle with the grated cheese and lemon rind and serve.

Nutritional information per portion: Energy 126kcal/519kJ; Protein 6.7g; Carbohydrate 2.7g, of which sugars 1.9g; Fat 9.8g, of which saturates 3.3g; Cholesterol 104mg; Calcium 106mg; Fibre 1.4g; Sodium 102mg.

Green rice

This rice seldom features on menus in Mexican restaurants, but is often made in the home.

SERVES 4

2 fresh green chillies, preferably poblanos
1 small green (bell) pepper
200g/7oz/1 cup long grain white rice
1 garlic clove, roughly chopped
1 bunch each of coriander (cilantro) and parsley, stalks removed
475ml/16fl oz/2 cups chicken stock
30ml/2 tbsp vegetable oil
1 small onion, finely chopped
salt

1 Dry roast the chillies and green pepper in a griddle pan. Place in a plastic bag and set aside for 20 minutes.

2 Put the rice in a heatproof bowl, pour over boiling water and leave to stand for 20 minutes. Drain, rinse under cold water and drain. Peel off the chilli and pepper skins. Remove stalks, slit open and scrape out the seeds.

3 Put the vegetables and garlic in a food processor. Add the coriander and parsley to the processor, reserving some for the garnish. Pour in half the stock and process until smooth. Add the rest of the stock and process again.

4 Heat the oil in a pan, add the onion and rice and fry for 5 minutes over a moderate heat until the rice is golden and the onion translucent. Stir in the purée. Lower the heat, cover and cook for 25–30 minutes until the rice is just tender. Add salt and garnish with the herbs.

Nutritional information per portion: Energy 257kcal/1069kJ; Protein 5.4g; Carbohydrate 44.2g, of which sugars 3.6g; Fat 6.3g, of which saturates 0.7g; Cholesterol 0mg; Calcium 49mg; Fibre 1.4g; Sodium 8mg.

Yellow rice

Ground achiote seed gives this dish its striking colour and distinctive flavour.

SERVES 6

200g/7oz/1 cup long grain white rice
30ml/2 tbsp vegetable oil
5ml/1 tsp ground achiote seed (annatto powder)
1 small onion, finely chopped
2 garlic cloves, crushed
475ml/16fl oz/2 cups chicken stock
50g/2oz/1/3 cup drained pickled jalapeño chilli slices, chopped
salt
fresh coriander (cilantro) leaves, to garnish

1 Put the rice in a heatproof bowl, pour over boiling water to cover and leave to stand for 20 minutes. Drain, rinse under cold water and drain again.

2 Heat the oil in a pan, add the ground achiote seed (annatto powder) and cook for 2–3 minutes. Add the onion and garlic and cook for a further 3–4 minutes or until the onion is translucent. Stir in the rice and cook for 5 minutes.

3 Pour in the stock, mix well and bring to the boil. Lower the heat, cover with a tight-fitting lid and simmer for 25–30 minutes, until all the liquid has been absorbed.

4 Add the chopped jalapeños to the pan and stir to distribute them evenly. Add salt to taste, then spoon into a heated serving dish and garnish with the fresh coriander leaves. Serve immediately.

Nutritional information per portion: Energy 163kcal/679kJ; Protein 3.6g; Carbohydrate 27.6g, of which sugars 0.8g; Fat 4.1g, of which saturates 0.4g; Cholesterol 0mg; Calcium 19mg; Fibre 0.1g; Sodium 3mg.

Chayotes with corn and chillies

Chayotes are members of the squash family and have rather a bland taste. They marry extremely well with other ingredients, such as the corn and roasted jalapeños in this medley.

SERVES 6

4 fresh jalapeño chillies
3 *chayotes*
oil, for frying
1 red onion, finely chopped
3 garlic cloves, crushed
225g/8oz/1¹⁄₃ cups corn kernels, thawed
    if frozen
150g/5oz/²⁄₃ cup cream cheese
5ml/1 tsp salt (optional)
25g/1oz/¹⁄₃ cup freshly grated
    Parmesan cheese

1 Dry roast the fresh jalapeño chillies in a griddle pan, turning them frequently so that the skins blacken but do not burn. Place them in a plastic bag, tie the top securely, and set them aside for 20 minutes.

2 Meanwhile, peel the *chayotes*, cut them in half and remove the seed from each of them. Cut the flesh into 1cm/¹⁄₂ in cubes.

3 Heat the oil in a frying pan. Add the onion, garlic, *chayote* cubes and corn. Fry over a moderate heat for 10 minutes, stirring occasionally.

4 Remove the jalapeños from the bag, peel off the skins and remove any stems. Cut them in half, scrape out the seeds, then cut the flesh into strips.

5 Add the chillies and cream cheese to the pan, stirring gently, until the cheese melts. Place in a serving dish.

6 Stir in salt, if needed, then spoon into a warmed dish. Sprinkle with the cheese and serve. This makes a good accompaniment for cold roast meats.

Nutritional information per portion: Energy 251kcal/1044kJ; Protein 6.9g; Carbohydrate 13.8g, of which sugars 6.1g; Fat 19.1g, of which saturates 9.7g; Cholesterol 32mg; Calcium 161mg; Fibre 1.5g; Sodium 281mg.

Spinach salad

Young spinach leaves make a welcome change from lettuce and are excellent in salads. The roasted garlic is an inspired addition to the dressing.

SERVES 6

500g/1¼ lb baby spinach leaves
50g/2oz/⅓ cup sesame seeds
50g/2oz/¼ cup butter
30ml/2 tbsp olive oil
6 shallots, sliced
8 fresh serrano chillies, seeded and cut
   into strips
4 tomatoes, sliced

FOR THE DRESSING

6 roasted garlic cloves
120ml/4fl oz/½ cup white wine vinegar
2.5ml/½ tsp ground white pepper
1 bay leaf
2.5ml/½ tsp ground allspice
30ml/2 tbsp chopped fresh thyme,
   plus extra sprigs to garnish

1 Make the dressing. Remove the skins from the garlic when cool, then chop and combine with the vinegar, pepper, bay leaf, allspice and chopped thyme in a jar with a screw-top lid. Shake well, then refrigerate until needed.

2 Wash the spinach leaves and dry them in a salad spinner or clean dish towel. Put them in a plastic bag in the refrigerator.

3 Toast the sesame seeds in a dry frying pan, shaking frequently over a moderate heat until golden. Set aside. Heat the butter and oil in a frying pan. Fry the shallots for 4–5 minutes, until softened, then stir in the chilli strips and fry for 2–3 minutes more.

4 In a large bowl, layer the spinach with the shallot and chilli mixture, and the tomato slices. Pour over the dressing. Sprinkle with sesame seeds and serve, garnished with thyme sprigs.

Nutritional information per portion: Energy 209kcal/866kJ; Protein 7.2g; Carbohydrate 9.2g, of which sugars 6.7g; Fat 16.2g, of which saturates 5.5g; Cholesterol 18mg; Calcium 218mg; Fibre 3.9g; Sodium 170mg.

Chayote salad

Cool and refreshing, this salad is ideal on its own or with fish or chicken dishes. The soft flesh of the chayotes *absorbs the flavour of the dressing beautifully.*

SERVES 4

2 *chayotes*
2 firm tomatoes
1 small onion, finely chopped
finely sliced strips of fresh red and green
    chilli, to garnish

FOR THE DRESSING
2.5ml/¹/₂ tsp Dijon mustard
2.5ml/¹/₂ tsp ground anise
90ml/6 tbsp white wine vinegar
60ml/4 tbsp olive oil
salt and ground black pepper

1 Bring a pan of water to the boil. Peel the *chayotes*, cut them in half and remove the seeds. Add them to the boiling water. Lower the heat and simmer for 20 minutes or until the *chayotes* are tender. Drain and set them aside to cool.

2 Meanwhile, peel the tomatoes. Cut a cross in the base of each tomato. Place them in a heatproof bowl and pour over boiling water to cover. After 3 minutes, lift the tomatoes out on a slotted spoon and plunge them into a bowl of cold water. Drain. The skins will have begun to peel back from the crosses. Remove the skins completely and cut the tomatoes into wedges.

3 Make the dressing by combining all the ingredients in a screw-top jar. Close the lid tightly and shake the jar vigorously.

4 Cut the *chayotes* into wedges and place in a bowl with the tomato and onion. Pour over the dressing and serve garnished with strips of fresh red and green chilli.

Nutritional information per portion: Energy 104kcal/430kJ; Protein 1.4g; Carbohydrate 5.3g, of which sugars 4.4g; Fat 8.7g, of which saturates 1.4g; Cholesterol 0mg; Calcium 40mg; Fibre 1.8g; Sodium 24mg.

Caesar salad

Although widely regarded as an American classic, Caesar salad actually originated in Mexico. Pregnant women, young children and the elderly are advised to avoid eating raw egg.

SERVES 4

2 garlic cloves, peeled and left whole
60ml/4 tbsp extra virgin olive oil
4 slices of bread, crusts removed, cubed
1 cos or romaine lettuce, separated
    into leaves
6 drained canned anchovy fillets,
    halved lengthways
shavings of Parmesan cheese, to garnish

FOR THE DRESSING
1 egg
10ml/2 tsp Dijon mustard
generous dash of Worcestershire sauce
30ml/2 tbsp lemon juice
30ml/2 tbsp extra virgin olive oil
salt and ground black pepper

1 Cut one garlic clove in half and rub it around the inside of a salad bowl. Put the remaining garlic in a frying pan. Add the oil and heat gently for 5 minutes, then discard the garlic. Add the bread cubes to the oil and fry them until they are crisp on all sides. Drain on kitchen paper.

2 Line the salad bowl with the cos or romaine leaves. Distribute the anchovy fillet halves among the lettuce leaves. Toss the leaves to spread the flavour of the anchovies.

3 Crack the egg into a food processor or blender with the Dijon mustard, Worcestershire sauce and lemon juice. Season to taste with salt and pepper and process to blend briefly, then add the oil with the motor running.

4 Pour the dressing over the salad in the bowl and toss lightly. Add the garlic croûtons. Transfer to individual bowls or carry to the table in the salad bowl. Sprinkle over Parmesan shavings and serve.

Nutritional information per portion: Energy 198kcal/824kJ; Protein 5.6g; Carbohydrate 13.8g, of which sugars 1.7g; Fat 13.8g, of which saturates 2.1g; Cholesterol 50mg; Calcium 64mg; Fibre 0.9g; Sodium 400mg.

Jicama, chilli and lime salad

A very tasty, crisp vegetable, the jicama *is sometimes called the Mexican potato. Unlike potato, however, it can be eaten raw. This makes a good salad or an appetizer to serve with drinks.*

SERVES 4

1 *jicama*
2.5ml/¹⁄₂ tsp salt
2 fresh serrano chillies
2 limes

1 Peel the *jicama* with a potato peeler or knife, then cut it into 2cm/³⁄₄ in cubes. Put these in a large bowl, add the salt and toss well.

2 Cut the chillies in half, scrape out the seeds with a sharp knife, then cut the flesh into fine strips. Grate one of the limes thinly, removing only the coloured part of the skin, then cut the lime in half and squeeze the juice.

3 Add the chillies, lime rind and juice to the *jicama* and mix thoroughly to ensure that all the *jicama* cubes are coated. Cut the other lime into wedges.

4 Cover and chill for at least 1 hour before serving with lime wedges. If the salad is to be served as an appetizer with drinks, transfer the *jicama* cubes to little bowls and offer them with cocktail sticks for spearing.

Nutritional information per portion: Energy 73kcal/309kJ; Protein 2.1g; Carbohydrate 16.2g, of which sugars 1.4g; Fat 0.4g, of which saturates 0.1g; Cholesterol 0mg; Calcium 10mg; Fibre 1g; Sodium 12mg.

Nopalitos salad

Nopalitos – *strips of pickled cactus paddles – are sold in cans or jars, and are very useful for making quick and easy salads like this one.*

SERVES 4

300g/11oz/scant 2 cups drained
    canned *nopalitos*
1 red (bell) pepper
30ml/2 tbsp olive oil
2 garlic cloves, sliced
$^{1}/_{2}$ red onion, thinly sliced
120ml/4fl oz/$^{1}/_{2}$ cup cider vinegar
small bunch of fresh coriander (cilantro),
    chopped, to garnish
salt

1 Preheat the grill (broiler). Put the *nopalitos* in a bowl, cover with water and set aside for 30 minutes. Drain, replace the water and soak for 30 minutes.

2 Place the red pepper halves cut side down in a grill pan. Grill the peppers until the skins blister and char, then put the pepper halves in a strong plastic bag, tie the top securely to keep the steam in, and set aside for 20 minutes.

3 Heat the oil in a small frying pan and fry the garlic over a low heat until the slices start to turn golden. Using a slotted spoon, transfer them to a salad bowl. Pour the garlic-flavoured oil into a jug and set it aside to cool.

4 Add the red onion slices to the salad bowl, then pour over the vinegar. Remove the red pepper from the bag, peel off the skins, then cut the flesh into thin strips. Add to the salad bowl. Drain the *nopalitos* and add them to the salad, with the garlic-flavoured oil and a little salt, to taste. Toss lightly, then chill until needed. Sprinkle the coriander over just before serving.

Nutritional information per portion: Energy 101kcal/419kJ; Protein 1.6g; Carbohydrate 10.4g, of which sugars 9.6g; Fat 6.1g, of which saturates 0.8g; Cholesterol 0mg; Calcium 15mg; Fibre 2.5g; Sodium 6mg.

Desserts
and drinks

Mexicans have a really sweet tooth. Ever

since Hernán Cortés introduced sugar cane

to the country, sweetmeats have been very

much on the menu and the array of cakes

and pastries in a Mexican pastelería would

rival any display in a European cake shop.

Mexico also boasts a marvellous range of

warm and cold drinks, from rich hot

chocolates to margaritas.

Caramel custard

If you order "Flan" from the menu in Mexico you might be disconcerted if you were expecting a sponge case filled with fruit. This hugely popular dessert is actually a caramel custard.

SERVES 6

1 litre/1³⁄4 pints/4 cups milk
1 vanilla pod, split
6 eggs
115g/4oz/¹⁄2 cup sugar
5ml/1 tsp natural vanilla extract

FOR THE CARAMEL
175g/6oz/³⁄4 cup caster (superfine) sugar

1 Put six ramekins in a sink of hot water. Make the caramel. Spread out the caster sugar evenly on the bottom of a large pan. Heat it slowly, without stirring, tilting the pan backwards and forwards on the heat until the sugar melts.

2 Lift the heated ramekins or moulds out of the water and dry them quickly. Watch the melted sugar closely, and when it turns a rich golden colour, pour the mixture into the dishes and simply turn until they are coated, or brush the caramel over the insides of the dishes. Set them aside.

3 Preheat the oven to 180°C/350°F/Gas 4. Pour the milk into a pan, add the vanilla pod and bring the milk to just below boiling point. Pour it into a jug (pitcher) and set it aside to cool.

4 Put the eggs in a bowl, beat them lightly, then gradually beat in the sugar and vanilla extract. Remove the vanilla from the milk, then gradually mix the milk into the egg. Strain the egg mixture into the caramel-lined ramekins or moulds and stand them in a roasting pan. Pour boiling water into the pan until it comes halfway up the sides of the dishes, then carefully put the tin in the oven.

5 Bake the custards for about 40 minutes. The custards are done when a knife blade, inserted in one of them, comes out clean. Lift the dishes out of the water, let them cool, then chill for several hours.

6 To serve, run a round-bladed knife around the edge of each custard, place a dessert plate upside-down on top of the dish and turn the dish and plate over together. Lift off the dish. Some of the caramel will settle in a puddle around the custard, so it is important not to choose dessert dishes that are too shallow. Try serving these custards with fresh fruit.

Nutritional information per portion: Energy 272kcal/1152kJ; Protein 10.7g; Carbohydrate 43.3g, of which sugars 43.3g; Fat 7.7g, of which saturates 2.9g; Cholesterol 198mg; Calcium 198mg; Fibre 0g; Sodium 126mg.

Rice pudding

Rice is a popular dessert ingredient in Mexico. One way of serving it is to cook it in milk until soft and thick, then shape it into balls. These are coated in egg and breadcrumbs, fried in oil, then rolled in cinnamon sugar to make sweet treats.

SERVES 4

75g/3oz/¹/₂ cup raisins

75ml/5 tbsp dry sherry

90g/3¹/₂ oz/¹/₂ cup short grain (pudding) rice

3 or 4 strips of pared lemon peel

250ml/8fl oz/1 cup water

475ml/16fl oz/2 cups milk

225g/8oz/1 cup sugar

pinch of salt

1 cinnamon stick, about 7.5cm/3in long, plus 3 more to decorate

2 egg yolks

15g/¹/₂ oz/1 tbsp butter, diced

toasted flaked (sliced) almonds, to decorate

chilled orange segments, to serve

1 Put the raisins and dry sherry in a small pan. Heat gently until warm, then set the pan aside, which will allow the raisins to swell.

2 Mix the rice, lemon peel and water in a heavy pan and bring to the boil. Lower the heat, cover the pan and simmer for about 20 minutes. Remove the lemon peel.

3 Add the milk and the cinnamon to the pan, then stir until the rice has absorbed the milk. Stir in the sugar and salt. Add the egg yolks and butter. Stir until the butter has melted.

4 Drain the raisins and stir into the rice mixture. Cook for 2–3 minutes, top with the toasted flaked almonds and serve with the orange segments.

Nutritional information per portion: Energy 433kcal/1829kJ; Protein 5.8g; Carbohydrate 85.6g, of which sugars 65.7g; Fat 6.9g, of which saturates 3.3g; Cholesterol 112mg; Calcium 113mg; Fibre 0.5g; Sodium 68mg.

Almond pudding with custard

This dish may well date from the time of the French occupation of Mexico, for it bears a close resemblance to île flottante *– floating islands – although in that recipe the meringues are poached in the custard. It is very light, making it perfect to follow a substantial main course.*

SERVES 6

250ml/8fl oz/1 cup water
15g/¹/₂ oz sachet powdered gelatine
275g/10oz/1¹/₄ cups sugar
2.5ml/¹/₂ tsp almond essence
6 eggs, separated
pinch of salt
475ml/16fl oz/2 cups single (light) cream
2.5ml/¹/₂ tsp natural vanilla extract
ground cinnamon, for dusting

1 Pour the water into a pan and sprinkle the gelatine over the surface. When it has softened, add 225g/8oz/1 cup of the sugar and place the pan over a low heat. Stir until both the gelatine and the sugar have dissolved, then stir in the almond essence. Pour it into a bowl and chill until it starts to thicken.

2 Whisk the egg whites until they are stiff. Whisk the gelatine mixture until is frothy, then fold in the egg whites carefully. Chill until firm.

3 Meanwhile, make the custard. Put the egg yolks, remaining sugar and salt in a heavy non-stick pan. Stir in the cream and vanilla extract. Cook over a very low heat, stirring constantly until the custard thickens to a soft dropping consistency, just enough to coat the back of a wooden spoon.

4 Pour the custard into dessert bowls. Cover each with a piece of dampened greaseproof (waxed) paper until ready to serve to prevent the formation of a skin.

5 Serve each custard topped with a few spoonfuls of the meringue mixture and a sprinkle of cinnamon.

Nutritional information per portion: Energy 360kcal/1507kJ; Protein 8.9g; Carbohydrate 39.1g, of which sugars 39.1g; Fat 19.9g, of which saturates 10.7g; Cholesterol 232mg; Calcium 114mg; Fibre 0g; Sodium 94mg.

Churros

A churrera is traditionally used to make churros, but an icing bag fitted with a large star nozzle makes a good substitute.

MAKES ABOUT 24

350g/12oz/3 cups plain (all-purpose) flour
5ml/1 tsp baking powder
600ml/1 pint/2¹/2 cups water
2.5ml/¹/2 tsp salt
25g/1oz/3 tbsp soft dark brown sugar
2 egg yolks
oil, for deep frying
2 limes, cut in wedges
caster (superfine) sugar, for dusting

1 Sift the flour and baking powder into a bowl. Set aside. Bring the water to the boil in a pan and add the salt and sugar, stirring until dissolved. Remove from the heat.

2 Tip in the flour and baking powder. Beat until smooth. Beat in the egg yolks, one at a time, until the mixture is smooth and glossy. Set the batter aside to cool. Have ready a piping bag fitted with a large star nozzle.

3 Pour oil into a deep fryer or suitable pan to a depth of about 5cm/2in. Heat to 190°C/375°F, or until a cube of dried bread floats and turns golden after 1 minute.

4 Spoon the batter into the piping bag. Pipe five or six 10cm/4in lengths of the mixture into the hot oil, using a knife to slice off each length. Fry for 3–4 minutes or until golden brown. Drain the *churros* on kitchen paper while cooking successive batches, then arrange on a plate with the lime wedges, dust them with caster sugar and serve.

Nutritional information per churro: Energy 122kcal/517kJ; Protein 2.6g; Carbohydrate 21.4g, of which sugars 2.3g; Fat 3.5g, of which saturates 0.5g; Cholesterol 17mg; Calcium 38mg; Fibre 0.8g; Sodium 2mg.

Sopaipillas

These golden pillows of puff pastry can be served as a dessert, with honey, or plain with soups. They are also ideal for finger buffets.

MAKES ABOUT 30

225g/8oz/2 cups plain (all-purpose) flour
15ml/1 tsp baking powder
5ml/1 tsp salt
25g/1oz/2 tbsp white cooking fat or margarine
175ml/6fl oz/³/4 cup warm water
oil, for deep frying
clear honey, for drizzling
ground cinnamon, for sprinkling
crème fraîche or double (heavy) cream, to serve

1 Sift the flour, baking powder and salt into a bowl. Rub in the fat or margarine until the mixture resembles fine breadcrumbs. Add water to form a dough. Wrap the dough in clear film (plastic wrap) and leave for 1 hour.

2 Working with half the dough at a time, roll it out to a square, keeping it as even and as thin as possible. Cut into 7.5cm/3in squares. When both pieces of the dough have been rolled and cut, set the squares aside.

3 Heat the oil for deep frying to 190°C/375°F, or until a cube of dried bread floats and turns golden after 1 minute. Add a few pastry squares, using tongs to push them down into the oil. Cook in batches until golden on both sides, turning them once, and drain on kitchen paper.

4 When all the *sopaipillas* have been cooked, arrange on a serving plate, drizzle with honey and sprinkle with cinnamon. Serve warm, with crème fraîche or cream.

Nutritional information per item: Energy 79kcal/332kJ; Protein 1.3g; Carbohydrate 12.9g, of which sugars 2.8g; Fat 2.8g, of which saturates 0.2g; Cholesterol 0mg; Calcium 19mg; Fibre 0.4g; Sodium 9mg.

Buñuelos

These lovely little puffs look like miniature doughnuts and taste so good it is hard not to over-indulge. Make them for brunch, or serve them with a cup of Café con Leche *or* Café de Olla.

MAKES 12

225g/8oz/2 cups plain (all-purpose) flour
pinch of salt
5ml/1 tsp baking powder
2.5ml/¹⁄₂ tsp ground anise
115g/4oz/¹⁄₂ cup caster (superfine)
    sugar

1 large egg
120ml/4fl oz/¹⁄₂ cup milk
50g/2oz/¹⁄₄ cup butter
oil, for deep frying
10ml/2 tsp ground cinnamon
cinnamon sticks, to decorate

1 Sift the flour, salt, baking powder and ground anise into a mixing bowl. Add 30ml/2 tbsp of the caster sugar. Place the egg and milk in a small jug and whisk well with a fork. Melt the butter in a small pan.

2 Pour the egg mixture and milk gradually into the flour, stirring all the time, until well blended, then add the melted butter. Mix first with a wooden spoon and then with your hands to make a soft dough.

3 Lightly flour a work surface, tip out the dough on to it and knead for about 10 minutes, until smooth. Divide the dough into 12 pieces and roll into balls. Slightly flatten each ball with your hand and then make a hole in the centre with the floured handle of a wooden spoon.

4 Heat the oil for deep frying to a temperature of 190°C/375°F, or until a cube of dried bread, added to the oil, floats and then turns a golden colour in 30–60 seconds. Fry the *buñuelos* in batches until they are puffy and golden brown, turning them once or twice during cooking. As soon as they are golden, lift them out of the oil using a slotted spoon and lie them on a double layer of kitchen paper to drain.

5 Mix the remaining caster sugar with the ground cinnamon in a small bowl. Add the *buñuelos*, one at a time, while they are still warm, toss them in the mixture until they are lightly coated and either serve at once or leave to cool. Decorate with cinnamon sticks.

Nutritional information per bun: Energy 169kcal/715kJ; Protein 4g; Carbohydrate 34.1g, of which sugars 8.7g; Fat 2.8g, of which saturates 1.4g; Cholesterol 21mg; Calcium 63mg; Fibre 1g; Sodium 24mg.

Pumpkin in brown sugar

Although pumpkin is a vegetable of the winter squash family, when sweetened and spiced it makes a rich, delicious dessert that looks very attractive and is not at all difficult to prepare.

SERVES 6

1 small pumpkin, about 800g/1³/₄ lb

350g/12oz/1¹/₂ cups soft dark brown
    sugar

120ml/4fl oz/¹/₂ cup water

5ml/1 tsp ground cloves

12 cinnamon sticks, each about
    10cm/4in long

fresh mint sprigs, to decorate

thick yogurt or crème fraîche, to serve

1 Halve the pumpkin, remove the seeds and fibres and cut into wedges. Arrange in a single layer in a heavy pan. Fill the hollows with the sugar.

2 Pour the water into the pan, taking care not to wash all the sugar to the bottom. Make sure that some of the water trickles down to the bottom to prevent the pumpkin from burning. Sprinkle on the ground cloves and add two of the cinnamon sticks.

3 Cover the pan and cook over a low heat for about 30 minutes, or until the pumpkin is tender and the sugar and water have formed a syrup. Check the pan occasionally to make sure that the pumpkin does not dry out or catch on the bottom.

4 Transfer the pumpkin to a platter and pour the hot syrup over. Decorate with mint and cinnamon sticks and serve with yogurt or crème fraîche.

Nutritional information per portion: Energy 184kcal/783kJ; Protein 1.3g; Carbohydrate 46.9g, of which sugars 46.1g; Fat 0.3g, of which saturates 0.2g; Cholesterol 0mg; Calcium 66mg; Fibre 1.5g; Sodium 3mg.

Coconut custard

Light and creamy, this is the perfect pudding for serving after a spicy main course. Children like it, and it is ideal for entertaining as it can be made ahead of time and kept in the fridge overnight.

SERVES 6

225g/8oz/1 cup sugar
250ml/8fl oz/1 cup water
1 cinnamon stick, about 7.5cm/3in long
175g/6oz/2 cups desiccated (dry
    unsweetened shredded) coconut
750ml/1¼ pints/3 cups milk
4 eggs
175ml/6fl oz/¾ cup whipping cream
50g/2oz/½ cup chopped almonds,
    toasted
strips of orange rind, to decorate

1 To make the cinnamon syrup, place the sugar and water in a very large pan, add the cinnamon stick and bring to the boil. Lower the heat and simmer the syrup, uncovered, for 5 minutes.

2 Add the coconut and cook over a low heat, stirring occasionally, for 5 minutes. Stir in the milk until the mixture has thickened slightly. Remove the cinnamon stick and remove from the heat.

3 Whisk the eggs until light and fluffy. Gradually incorporate the coconut mixture, then scrape into a clean pan.

4 Cook over a low heat, stirring constantly, until the mixture becomes a thick custard. Cool, then chill. Just before serving, whip the cream. Transfer to individual bowls, top with the cream, almonds and orange rind and serve. Toasted flaked almonds also go well with this.

Nutritional information per portion: Energy 433kcal/1792kJ; Protein 10.2g; Carbohydrate 7.8g, of which sugars 7.8g; Fat 40.5g, of which saturates 29g; Cholesterol 170mg; Calcium 168mg; Fibre 4.6g; Sodium 108mg.

Fruit platter with chilli and lime

Any fruits that are in season can be used to make this refreshing dessert.

SERVES 6

$1/2$ small watermelon
2 mangoes and 2 papayas
1 small pineapple
1 fresh coconut
1 *jicama*
juice of 2 limes, plus lime wedges to serve
sea salt and mild red chilli powder

1 Slice the watermelon, then cut each slice into bite-size triangles and remove the seeds. Take a slice off the stone on the side of each mango, then cross-hatch the flesh. Turn the slices inside out and slice off the cubes of flesh.

2 Halve and seed the payayas and cut into wedges, leaving the skin on. Cut the top and base off the pineapple. Remove the skin and "eyes" with a knife using a spiral action. Cut the pineapple lengthways in quarters and remove the core. Slice each piece into wedges.

3 Make a hole in two of the "eyes" of the coconut, using a nail and hammer. Pour out the liquid. Tap the coconut with a hammer until it breaks. Remove the shell, then use a potato peeler to remove the brown layer. Cut into pieces.

4 Peel and slice the *jicama*. Arrange all the fruits on a platter, sprinkle them with lime juice and serve with lime wedges and bowls of salt and chilli powder for sprinkling.

Nutritional information per portion: Energy 232kcal/975kJ; Protein 2.6g; Carbohydrate 32.9g, of which sugars 32.8g; Fat 11g, of which saturates 9g; Cholesterol 0mg; Calcium 54mg; Fibre 7.4g; Sodium 15mg.

Ice cream with Mexican chocolate

This dessert has a complex flavour, thanks to the cinnamon and almonds in Mexican chocolate.

SERVES 4

2 large eggs
115g/4oz/$1/2$ cup caster (superfine) sugar
2 bars Mexican chocolate, total weight
    about 115g/4oz (about 2 discs)
400ml/14fl oz/$1^2/3$ cups double (heavy) cream
200ml/7fl oz/scant 1 cup milk
chocolate curls, to decorate

1 Put the eggs in a bowl and whisk them with an electric whisk until they are thick, pale and fluffy. Gradually whisk in the sugar.

2 Melt the chocolate in a heavy pan over a low heat, then add it to the egg mixture and mix thoroughly. Whisk in the cream, then stir in the milk, a little at a time. Cool the mixture, then chill. Pour the mixture into an ice-cream maker and churn until thick.

3 Alternatively, freeze it in a shallow plastic box in the fast-freeze section of the freezer for several hours, until ice crystals have begun to form around the edges. Process to break up the ice crystals, then freeze again. To serve, decorate with chocolate curls.

Nutritional information per portion: Energy 710kcal/2949kJ; Protein 7.6g; Carbohydrate 43.2g, of which sugars 43g; Fat 57.6g, of which saturates 34.7g; Cholesterol 220mg; Calcium 137mg; Fibre 0.6g; Sodium 79mg.

Capirotada

This pudding was invented as a way of using up food before the Lenten fast, but it is now eaten at other times too.

SERVES 6

1 small French stick, a few days old
115g/4oz/1/2 cup butter, softened, plus extra for greasing
200g/7oz/scant 1 cup soft dark brown sugar
1 cinnamon stick, about 15cm/6in long
400ml/14fl oz/1²/₃ cups water
45ml/3 tbsp dry sherry
75g/3oz/³/4 cup flaked (sliced) almonds, plus extra, to decorate
75g/3oz/1/2 cup raisins
115g/4oz/1 cup grated Monterey Jack or mild Cheddar cheese
single (heavy) cream, for pouring

1 Slice the bread into 30 rounds, each 1cm/1/2in thick. Lightly butter on both sides. Cook in batches in a warm frying pan until browned, turning over once. Set aside.

2 Place the sugar, cinnamon and water in a pan. Heat gently, stirring all the time, until the sugar has dissolved. Bring to the boil, then lower the heat and simmer for 15 minutes without stirring. Remove the cinnamon stick, then stir in the sherry.

3 Preheat the oven to 180°C/350°F/Gas 4. Grease a 20cm/8in square baking dish with butter. Layer the bread rounds, almonds, raisins and cheese in the dish, pour the syrup over, letting it soak into the bread. Bake the pudding for about 30 minutes until golden brown.

4 Remove from the oven, leave to stand for 5 minutes, then cut into squares. Serve cold, with cream poured over and decorated with the extra flaked almonds.

Nutritional information per portion: Energy 498kcal/2085kJ; Protein 13.7g;
Carbohydrate 47.7g, of which sugars 11.9g; Fat 28g, of which saturates 13.4g;
Cholesterol 53mg; Calcium 256mg; Fibre 2.8g; Sodium 655mg.

Drunken plantain

Until their cuisine was influenced by Europe, Mexicans had no pastries or cakes, preferring to end their meals with fruit.

SERVES 6

3 ripe plantains
50g/2oz/1/4 cup butter, diced
45ml/3 tbsp rum
grated rind and juice of 1 small orange
5ml/1 tsp ground cinnamon
50g/2oz/1/4 cup soft dark brown sugar
50g/2oz/1/2 cup whole almonds, in their skins
fresh mint sprigs, to decorate
crème fraîche or thick double (heavy) cream, to serve

1 Preheat the oven to 180°C/350°F/Gas 4. Peel the plantains and cut them in half lengthways. Put the pieces in a shallow baking dish, dot them all over with butter, then spoon over the rum and orange juice.

2 Mix the orange rind, cinnamon and brown sugar in a bowl. Sprinkle the mixture over the plantains.

3 Bake for 25–30 minutes, until the plantains are soft and the sugar has melted into the rum and orange juice.

4 Meanwhile, slice the almonds and dry fry them in a heavy frying pan until the cut sides are golden. Serve the plantains in individual bowls, with some of the sauce spooned over. Sprinkle the almonds on top, decorate with the fresh mint sprigs and offer crème fraîche or double cream separately.

Nutritional information per portion: Energy 240kcal/1006kJ; Protein 2.8g;
Carbohydrate 27.5g, of which sugars 15.4g; Fat 12.1g, of which saturates 4.8g;
Cholesterol 18mg; Calcium 43mg; Fibre 1.7g; Sodium 55mg.

Pecan cake

This cake is an example of the French influence on Mexican cooking. It is traditionally served with cajeta – sweetened boiled milk – but whipped cream or crème fraîche can be used instead.

SERVES 8–10

115g/4oz/1 cup pecan nuts
115g/4oz/1/2 cup butter, softened
115g/4oz/1/2 cup soft light brown sugar
5ml/1 tsp natural vanilla essence
4 large eggs, separated
75g/3oz/3/4 cup plain (all-purpose) flour
pinch of salt
12 whole pecan nuts, to decorate
cajeta, whipped cream or crème fraîche,
   to serve

FOR DRIZZLING

50g/2oz/1/4 cup butter
120ml/4fl oz/scant 1/2 cup clear honey

1 Preheat the oven to 180°C/350°F/Gas 4. Grease a 20cm/8in round spring-form cake pan. Toast the pecan nuts in a dry frying pan for 5 minutes, shaking frequently. Grind finely into a blender or food processor. Place in a bowl.

2 Cream the butter with the sugar in a mixing bowl, then beat in the vanilla essence and egg yolks.

3 Add the flour to the ground nuts and mix well. Whisk the egg whites with the salt in a grease-free bowl until soft peaks form. Fold the whites into the butter mixture, then gently fold in the flour and nut mixture. Spoon the mixture into the prepared cake tin and bake for 30 minutes or until a skewer inserted in the centre comes out clean. Cool the cake in the tin for 5 minutes, then remove the sides of the tin. Stand the cake on a wire rack until cold.

4 Remove the cake from the base of the tin, then return it to the rack and arrange the pecans on top. Transfer to a plate. Melt the butter in a small pan, add the honey and bring to the boil, stirring. Lower the heat and simmer for 3 minutes. Pour over the cake. Serve with *cajeta*, cream or crème fraîche.

Nutritional information per portion: Energy 404kcal/1684kJ; Protein 5.9g; Carbohydrate 37g, of which sugars 23.5g; Fat 26.8g, of which saturates 9.5g; Cholesterol 108mg; Calcium 55mg; Fibre 1.4g; Sodium 122mg.

Garbanzo cake

This is a moist cake, with a texture like that of Christmas pudding. It is flavoured with orange and cinnamon and tastes wonderful in thin slices, with mango or pineapple and a spoonful of yogurt.

SERVES 6

2 x 275g/10oz cans chickpeas, drained
4 eggs, beaten
225g/8oz/1 cup caster (superfine) sugar
5ml/1 tsp baking powder
10ml/2 tsp ground cinnamon
grated rind and juice of 1 orange

FOR THE CINNAMON SUGAR
50g/2oz/¼ cup caster (superfine) sugar
15ml/1 tsp ground cinnamon

1 Preheat the oven to 180°C/350°F/Gas 4. Tip the chickpeas into a colander, drain them thoroughly, then rub them between the palms of your hands to loosen and remove the skins. Put the skinned chickpeas in a food processor and process until smooth.

2 Spoon the purée into a bowl and stir in the eggs, sugar, baking powder, cinnamon, orange rind and juice. Grease and line a 450g/1lb loaf tin (pan).

3 Pour the cake mixture into the loaf tin, level the surface and bake for about 1½ hours or until a skewer inserted into the centre comes out clean.

4 Remove the cake from the oven and leave to stand, in the tin, for about 10 minutes. Meanwhile, mix the sugar and cinnamon. Remove the cake from the tin, place on a wire rack and sprinkle with the cinnamon sugar. Leave to cool completely before serving. Try serving this with sliced fresh pineapple.

Nutritional information per portion: Energy 344kcal/1455kJ; Protein 14.1g; Carbohydrate 57.9g, of which sugars 39.1g; Fat 7.9g, of which saturates 1.6g; Cholesterol 152mg; Calcium 104mg; Fibre 5.3g; Sodium 323mg.

Almond biscuits

Icing sugar and butter combine to give these biscuits a light, delicate texture. They can be made days ahead, and are delicious with desserts or coffee.

MAKES ABOUT 24

115g/4oz/1 cup plain (all-purpose) flour
175g/6oz/1½ cups icing (confectioners')
sugar
pinch of salt
50g/2oz/½ cup chopped almonds
2.5ml/½ tsp almond essence
115g/4oz/½ cup unsalted butter,
softened
icing sugar, for dusting
halved almonds, to decorate

1 Preheat the oven to 180°C/350°F/Gas 4. Combine the flour, sugar, salt and chopped almonds in a bowl. Add the almond essence.

2 Put the softened butter in the centre of the flour mixture and use a knife or your fingertips to draw the dry ingredients into the butter until a dough is formed. Shape the dough into a ball.

3 Place the dough on a lightly floured surface and roll it out to a thickness of about 3mm/⅛ in. Using a 7.5cm/3in biscuit cutter, cut out about 24 rounds, re-rolling the dough as necessary.

4 Place the rounds on baking sheets, leaving a little space between them. Bake for 25–30 minutes until pale golden.

5 Leave for 10 minutes, then transfer to wire racks to cool. Dust thickly with sugar before serving, decorated with halved almonds.

Nutritional information per biscuit: Energy 115kcal/481kJ; Protein 1.5g; Carbohydrate 15g, of which sugars 10.1g; Fat 5.8g, of which saturates 2.4g; Cholesterol 9mg; Calcium 24mg; Fibre 0.5g; Sodium 27mg.

Pan dulce

These "sweet breads" of various shapes are made throughout Mexico, and can be eaten as a snack, a dessert or with jam or marmalade for breakfast.

MAKES 12

10ml/2 tsp active dried yeast
120ml/4fl oz/¹/₂ cup lukewarm milk
450g/1lb/4 cups strong plain (all-
    purpose) flour
75g/3oz/6 tbsp caster (superfine) sugar
25g/1oz/2 tbsp butter, softened
4 large eggs, beaten
oil, for greasing

FOR THE TOPPING
75g/3oz/6 tbsp butter, softened
115g/4oz/¹/₂ cup sugar
1 egg yolk
5ml/1 tsp ground cinnamon
115g/4oz/1 cup plain (all-purpose) flour

1 In a bowl, stir the yeast into the milk and leave in a warm place until frothy.

2 Put the flour and sugar in a mixing bowl, add the butter and beaten eggs and mix to a soft, sticky dough. Place the dough on a lightly floured surface and dredge it with more flour. Using floured hands, turn the dough over and over until it is completely covered in a light coating of flour. Cover it with lightly oiled clear film (plastic wrap) and leave to rest for 20 minutes.

3 Cream the butter and sugar in a bowl. Mix in the other topping ingredients.

4 Divide the dough into 12 equal pieces and shape into rounds. Space well apart on greased baking sheets. Sprinkle the topping over the breads, dividing it more or less equally among them, then press it lightly into the surface.

5 Leave the bread in a warm place to stand for 30 minutes. Preheat the oven to 200°C/400°F/Gas 6 and bake for about 15 minutes.

Nutritional information per bun: Energy 358kcal/1510kJ; Protein 6.5g; Carbohydrate 65.2g, of which sugars 17.6g; Fat 9.6g, of which saturates 5.6g; Cholesterol 39mg; Calcium 110mg; Fibre 1.9g; Sodium 68mg.

Wedding cookies

These delicious little shortbread biscuits are traditionally served at weddings in Mexico.

MAKES 30

225g/8oz/1 cup butter, softened
175g/6oz/1¹/₂ cups icing (confectioners') sugar
5ml/1 tsp natural vanilla essence
300g/11oz/2³/₄ cups plain (all-purpose) flour
pinch of salt
150g/5oz/1¹/₄ cups pecan nuts, finely chopped

1 Preheat the oven to 190°C/375°F/Gas 5. Beat the butter in a large bowl until it is light and fluffy, then beat in 115g/4oz/1 cup of the icing sugar, with the vanilla essence.

2 Gradually add the flour and salt to the creamed mixture until it starts to form a dough. Add the finely chopped pecans with the remaining flour. Knead the dough lightly.

3 Divide the dough into 30 pieces and roll them into balls. Space about 5mm/¹/₄ in apart on baking sheets. Flatten each ball slightly with your thumb.

4 Bake the biscuits for 10–15 minutes until they are starting to brown. Cool on the baking sheets for 10 minutes, then transfer to wire racks to cool completely.

5 Put the remaining sugar in a bowl. Add a few biscuits at a time, shaking them in the sugar until they are coated. Serve immediately or store in an airtight tin.

Nutritional information per cookie: Energy 117kcal/490kJ; Protein 1.5g; Carbohydrate 16.9g, of which sugars 7.3g; Fat 5.2g, of which saturates 2g; Cholesterol 7mg; Calcium 24mg; Fibre 0.5g; Sodium 21mg.

Almond orange biscuits

The combination of lard and almonds gives these biscuits a melt-in-the-mouth texture.

MAKES 36

250g/9oz/generous 1 cup lard
125g/4¹/₂ oz/generous ¹/₂ cup caster (superfine) sugar
2 eggs, beaten
grated rind and juice of 1 small orange
300g/11oz/1³/₄ cups plain (all-purpose) flour, sifted with
   5ml/1 tsp baking powder
200g/7oz/1³/₄ cups ground almonds

FOR DUSTING
50g/2oz/¹/₂ cup icing (confectioners') sugar
5ml/1 tsp ground cinnamon

1 Preheat the oven to 200°C/400°F/Gas 6. Place the lard in a large bowl and beat with an electric whisk until light and aerated. Gradually beat in the caster sugar.

2 Continue to whisk the mixture while you add the eggs, orange rind and juice. Whisk for 3–4 minutes more, then stir in the flour mixture and almonds to form a dough.

3 Roll out the dough on a lightly floured surface until it is about 1cm/¹/₂ in thick. Using biscuit cutters, cut out 36 rounds, re-rolling the dough if necessary. Gently lift the rounds on to greased baking sheets.

4 Bake for about 10 minutes, or until the biscuits are golden. Leave to stand for 10 minutes to cool and firm.

5 Mix together the icing sugar and cinnamon. Put the mixture in a small sieve or tea strainer and dust the biscuits well. Leave to cool completely before serving.

Nutritional information per biscuit: Energy 131kcal/546kJ; Protein 2.3g; Carbohydrate 9.5g, of which sugars 3.5g; Fat 9.6g, of which saturates 2.9g; Cholesterol 16mg; Calcium 28mg; Fibre 0.7g; Sodium 5mg.

Christmas cookies with walnuts

At Christmas time, these cookies are individually wrapped in small squares of brightly coloured tissue paper and arranged in large bowls.

MAKES 24

115g/4oz/¹/₂ cup lard or white cooking fat, softened and diced
75g/3oz/³/₄ cup icing (confectioners') sugar
5ml/1 tsp vanilla essence
150g/5oz/1¹/₄ cups unbleached plain (all-purpose) flour
75g/3oz/³/₄ cup broken walnuts, finely chopped
50g/2oz/¹/₂ cup icing sugar
10ml/2 tsp ground cinnamon

1 Preheat the oven to 190°C/375°F/Gas 5. Place the lard in a large bowl and beat with an electric whisk until light and aerated. Gradually beat in 25g/1oz/¹/₄ cup of the icing sugar, then add the vanilla essence and beat well.

2 Add the flour by hand, working it gently into the mixture. Add the walnuts and mix carefully.

3 Divide the dough evenly into 24 small pieces, roll each to a ball, and space well apart on baking sheets. Bake for 10–15 minutes, until golden, switching the baking sheets around halfway through, to ensure even baking. Cool on wire racks.

4 Put the remaining sugar in a bowl and stir in the cinnamon. Add a few biscuits at a time, shaking them in the icing sugar until they are heavily coated. Shake off the excess sugar. Serve wrapped in coloured paper.

Nutritional information per cookie: Energy 141kcal/591kJ; Protein 1.7g; Carbohydrate 15.4g, of which sugars 9g; Fat 8.5g, of which saturates 2g; Cholesterol 4mg; Calcium 22mg; Fibre 0.5g; Sodium 1mg.

Fruit-filled empanadas

Imagine biting through crisp buttery pastry to discover a rich fruity filling flavoured with oranges and cinnamon. These are the stuff that dreams are made of.

MAKES 12

275g/10oz/2½ cups plain (all-purpose) flour
25g/1oz/2 tbsp sugar
90g/3½ oz/scant ½ cup chilled butter, cubed
1 egg yolk
iced water (see method)
milk, to glaze
caster (superfine) sugar, for sprinkling
almonds and orange wedges, to serve

FOR THE FILLING

25g/1oz/2 tbsp butter
3 ripe plantains, peeled and mashed
5ml/1 tsp ground cinnamon
2.5ml/½ tsp ground cloves
225g/8oz/1⅓ cups raisins
grated rind and juice of 2 oranges

1 Combine the flour and sugar in a bowl. Rub in the chilled cubes of butter until the mixture resembles fine breadcrumbs. Beat the egg yolk and add to the mixture. Add iced water to make a smooth dough. Shape it into a ball.

2 Melt the butter for the filling in a pan. Add the plantains, cinnamon and cloves and cook over a moderate heat for 2–3 minutes. Stir in the raisins, rind and juice. Lower the heat so that the mixture barely simmers. Cook for 15 minutes, until the raisins are plump and the juice has evaporated. Leave to cool.

3 Preheat the oven to 200°C/400°F/Gas 6. Roll out the pastry on a lightly floured surface. Cut it into 10cm/4in rounds. Place the rounds on a baking sheet and spoon on a little of the filling. Dampen the rim of the pastry rounds with water, fold the pastry over the filling and crimp the edges to seal.

4 Brush the pastries with milk and bake them for 15 minutes or until golden. Sprinkle with sugar and serve warm, with whole almonds and orange wedges.

Nutritional information per empanada: Energy 276kcal/1161kJ; Protein 4g; Carbohydrate 45.4g, of which sugars 15.7g; Fat 9.9g, of which saturates 5.9g; Cholesterol 40mg; Calcium 59mg; Fibre 1.7g; Sodium 80mg.

Kings' Day bread

This bread is an important part of the Twelfth Night celebrations. A doll and a bean are hidden inside, and the parents of the children who find them have to host a party on February 2nd.

SERVES 8

120ml/4fl oz/¹/₂ cup lukewarm water
10ml/2 tsp active dried yeast
6 eggs
275g/10oz/2¹/₂ cups plain (all-purpose) flour
2.5ml/¹/₂ tsp salt
50g/2oz/¹/₄ cup sugar
115g/4oz/¹/₂ cup butter, plus 25g/1oz/

2 tbsp melted butter, for glazing
225g/8oz/1¹/₂ cups crystallized fruit and candied peel
175g/6oz/1¹/₂ cups icing (confectioners') sugar, plus extra for dusting
30ml/2 tbsp single (light) cream
crystallized fruit and glacé (candied) cherries, to decorate

1 Pour the water into a small bowl, stir in the dried yeast and leave in a warm place until frothy. Crack four of the eggs and divide the yolks from the whites. Place the four yolks in a small bowl and discard the egg whites.

2 Put 150g/5oz/1¹/₄ cups of the flour in a mixing bowl. Add the salt and sugar. Break the remaining two eggs into the bowl, then add the four egg yolks. Add 115g/4oz/¹/₂ cup of the butter to the bowl together with the yeast and water mixture. Mix all the ingredients together well.

3 Put the crystallized fruit and peel into a separate bowl. Add 50g/2oz/¹/₂ cup of the remaining flour and toss the fruit with the flour to coat it.

4 Add the floured fruit to the egg mixture, with the rest of the flour. Mix to a soft, non-sticky dough. Knead the dough on a lightly floured surface for about 10 minutes, until smooth. Shape the dough into a ball. Using the floured handle of a wooden spoon, make a hole in the centre, and enlarge. Put the dough ring onto a greased baking sheet and cover lightly with oiled clear film (plastic wrap). Leave in a warm place for about 2 hours or until doubled in bulk.

5 Preheat the oven to 180°C/350°F/Gas 4. Brush the dough with the melted butter and bake for about 30 minutes or until it has risen well and is cooked through and springy. Mix the icing sugar and cream in a bowl. Drizzle the mixture over the bread when it is cool and decorate it with the crystallized fruit and glacé cherries. Dust with icing sugar.

Nutritional information per portion: Energy 468kcal/1978kJ; Protein 9.5g; Carbohydrate 84g, of which sugars 48.3g; Fat 12.9g, of which saturates 6.3g; Cholesterol 163mg; Calcium 141mg; Fibre 2.7g; Sodium 180mg.

Tequila slammer

Mexicans have long enjoyed the taste of lime and salt with their food and drink. Beer is also taken with lime and salt. This is how to drink a tequila slammer.

SERVES 1

30ml/2 tbsp chilled tequila
salt
wedge of lime

1 Pour a shot of tequila into a glass. Lick the space between the thumb and the index finger on your left hand, then sprinkle this area with salt, taking care not to spill it.

2 Hold a lime wedge in the same hand as the salt. Pick up the shot glass. Lick the salt, down the tequila in one, suck the lime, then slam down your empty glass.

Nutritional information per portion: Energy 111kcal/460kJ; Protein 0g; Carbohydrate 0g, of which sugars 0g; Fat 0g, of which saturates 0g; Cholesterol 0mg; Calcium 0mg; Fibre 0g; Sodium 0mg.

Tequila sunrise

This drink takes its name from the way the grenadine – a bright red cordial made from pomegranate juice – first sinks in the glass of orange juice and then rises to the surface.

SERVES 1

25ml/1¹/₂ tbsp golden tequila
60ml/4 tbsp freshly squeezed orange juice
juice of 1 lime
5ml/1 tsp grenadine

1 Half fill a cocktail glass with crushed ice. Pour in the tequila, then the orange and lime juices, which should be freshly squeezed, not concentrated or bottled.

2 Quickly add the grenadine, pouring it down the back of a teaspoon held in the glass so that it sinks to the bottom of the drink. Serve immediately.

Nutritional information per portion: Energy 88kcal/369kJ; Protein 0.3g; Carbohydrate 6.5g, of which sugars 6.5g; Fat 0.1g, of which saturates 0g; Cholesterol 0mg; Calcium 6mg; Fibre 0.1g; Sodium 6mg.

Pineapple tequila

Many ingredients can be added to blanco tequila to create different flavours. Here, adding pineapple makes a smooth fruity drink. Almond or quince are also popular additions.

SERVES 6

1 large pineapple
50g/2oz soft dark brown sugar
1 litre blanco tequila
1 vanilla pod

1 Rinse a large (about 2 litre/3½ pint) wide-necked bottle or demijohn and sterilize by placing it in an oven and then turning on the oven and setting it at 110°C/225°F/Gas ¼. After 20 minutes remove the bottle from the oven with oven gloves and allow to cool.

2 Cut the top off the pineapple and cut away the skin, being careful to get rid of all the scales. Cut in half, remove the centre core and discard it. Chop the rest of the pineapple into chunks small enough to fit in the bottle neck.

3 When the bottle is completely cold, put the pineapple into the bottle. Mix the sugar and tequila together in a jug until the sugar dissolves and then pour into the bottle. Split the vanilla pod and add it to the bottle.

4 Gently agitate the bottle a few times each day to stir the contents. Allow the tequila to stand for at least 1 week before drinking.

Nutritional information per portion: Energy 406kcal/1686kJ; Protein 0.1g; Carbohydrate 9.6g, of which sugars 9.6g; Fat 0g, of which saturates 0g; Cholesterol 0mg; Calcium 5mg; Fibre 0g; Sodium 1mg.

Margarita

The most renowned tequila cocktail, this can be served over ice cubes or "frozen" – mixed with crushed ice in a cocktail shaker to create a liquid sorbet effect, then poured into the glass.

SERVES 1

45ml/3 tbsp tequila
25ml/1¹/₂ tbsp triple sec
25ml/1¹/₂ tbsp freshly squeezed
    lime juice
crushed ice or ice cubes
lime wedge and salt, for frosting glass

1 Frost a cocktail glass by rubbing the outer rim with the wedge of lime. Dip the glass in a saucer of salt so that it is evenly coated. It is important that there is no salt inside the glass, so take care that lime juice is only applied to the outer rim.

2 Combine the tequila, triple sec and lime juice in a cocktail shaker, add crushed ice, if using, and shake to mix. Carefully pour into the frosted glasses. If crushed ice is not used, place ice cubes in the glass and then pour the mixture over.

Nutritional information per portion: Energy 160kcal/668kJ; Protein 0.1g; Carbohydrate 7.7g, of which sugars 7.7g; Fat 0g, of which saturates 0g; Cholesterol 0mg; Calcium 3mg; Fibre 0g; Sodium 3mg.

Mango and peach margarita

Adding puréed fruit to the classic tequila mixture alters the consistency and makes for a glorious drink that resembles a milkshake but packs considerably more punch.

SERVES 4

2 mangoes, peeled and sliced
3 peaches, peeled and sliced
120ml/4fl oz / ½ cup tequila
60ml/4 tbsp triple sec
60ml/4 tbsp freshly squeezed lime juice
10 ice cubes, crushed, if necessary
mango slices, skin on, to decorate

1 Place the mango and peach slices in a food processor or blender. Process or blend until all the fruit is finely chopped.

2 Scrape down the sides of the goblet, then blend again until the purée is perfectly smooth.

3 Add the tequila, triple sec and lime juice, process or blend briefly, then add the ice. Repeat until the drink has the consistency of a milkshake.

4 Pour the drink into cocktail glasses, decorate with the mango slices and serve.

Nutritional information per portion: Energy 179kcal/754kJ; Protein 1.1g; Carbohydrate 19.1g, of which sugars 18.9g; Fat 0.2g, of which saturates 0.1g; Cholesterol 0mg; Calcium 13mg; Fibre 2.7g; Sodium 4mg.

Licuado de melon

Among the most refreshing drinks Mexicans make are fruit extracts mixed with honey and chilled water. This recipe uses watermelon and limes to create a delicious summer drink.

SERVES 4

1 watermelon
1 litre/1¾ pints/4 cups chilled water
juice of 2 limes
honey, to taste
ice cubes, to serve

1 Cut the watermelon flesh into chunks, cutting away the skin and discarding the shiny black seeds.

2 Place the watermelon chunks in a large bowl, pour over the chilled water and leave the mixture to stand for 10 minutes.

3 Tip the mixture into a large sieve set over a bowl. Using a wooden spoon, press gently on the fruit to extract all the liquid. Stir in the lime juice and sweeten with honey.

4 Pour into a jug, add ice cubes and stir. Serve in tumblers.

Nutritional information per portion: Energy 35kcal/155kJ; Protein 2g; Carbohydrate 7.5g, of which sugars 7.5g; Fat 0g, of which saturates 0g; Cholesterol 0mg; Calcium 25mg; Fibre 1.5g; Sodium 575mg.

Citrus agua fresca

These refreshing fruit juices are sold from street stalls in towns all over Mexico. The varieties of fruit used change with the seasons.

SERVES 6

12 limes
3 oranges
2 grapefruit
600ml/1 pint/2¹/₂ cups water
75g/3oz/6 tbsp caster (superfine) sugar
extra fruit wedges, to decorate
ice cubes, to serve

1 Squeeze the juice from the limes, oranges and grapefruit. Some fruit pulp may collect along with the juice. If this happens, remove and discard any seeds from the pulp and then add the pulp to the liquid. Pour the mixture into a large jug.

2 Add the water and sugar and stir until all the sugar has dissolved.

3 Chill for at least 1 hour before serving with ice and fruit wedges. The drink will keep for up to 1 week in a covered container in the fridge.

Nutritional information per portion: Energy 119kcal/506kJ; Protein 0.5g; Carbohydrate 31g, of which sugars 31g; Fat 0.1g, of which saturates 0g; Cholesterol 0mg; Calcium 23mg; Fibre 0g; Sodium 9mg.

Lime agua fresca

This is the lime version of real English lemonade. Mexican limes – limones – are harder and more tart than the smooth-skinned varieties most often sold in Western supermarkets.

SERVES 6

1.75 litres/3 pints/7½ cups water
75g/3oz/6 tbsp caster (superfine) sugar
10 limes, plus slices to decorate
ice cubes, to serve

1 Pour the water into a large jug, add the sugar and stir until all the sugar has dissolved. Chill for at least 1 hour.

2 Using a zester or grater, remove the rind from the limes, taking care to take only the coloured zest, not the pith. Squeeze the juice from the limes and add this to the chilled sugar water with the lime rind. Stir well and chill again until required. Serve with ice in tall glasses, decorated with lime slices.

Nutritional information per portion: Energy 62kcal/263kJ; Protein 0.2g; Carbohydrate 16.2g, of which sugars 16.2g; Fat 0g, of which saturates 0g; Cholesterol 0mg; Calcium 10mg; Fibre 0g; Sodium 1mg.

Pineapple and lime agua fresca

The vivid colours of this fresh fruit drink give some indication of its wonderful flavour. It makes a delicious midday refresher or pick-me-up at the end of a hard day.

SERVES 4

2 pineapples
juice of 2 limes
475ml/16fl oz/2 cups still mineral water
50g/2oz/¼ cup caster (superfine) sugar
ice cubes, to serve

1 Peel the pineapples and chop the flesh, removing the core and "eyes". You should have about 450g/1lb flesh. Put this in a food processor or blender and add the lime juice and half the mineral water. Purée to a smooth pulp. Stop the machine and scrape the mixture from the sides of the goblet once or twice during processing.

2 Place a sieve (strainer) over a large bowl. Tip the pineapple pulp into the sieve and press it through with a wooden spoon. Pour the stained mixture into a large jug (pitcher), cover and chill in the fridge for about 1 hour.

3 Stir in the remaining mineral water and sugar to taste. Serve with ice.

Nutritional information per portion: Energy 125kcal/537kJ; Protein 0.5g; Carbohydrate 32.7g, of which sugars 32.7g; Fat 0.1g, of which saturates 0g; Cholesterol 0mg; Calcium 20mg; Fibre 0g; Sodium 11mg.

Tamarind agua fresca

Tamarind is native to Asia and North Africa. Seeds came to Mexico via India. It is used medicinally and as an antiseptic. The fruit has a sweet-sour taste and makes a drink similar to lemonade.

SERVES 4

1 litre/1¾ pints/4 cups water
225g/8oz tamarind pods
25g/1oz/2 tbsp caster (superfine) sugar
ice cubes, to serve

1 Pour the water into a pan and heat until warm. Remove from the heat and pour into a bowl. Peel the tamarind pods and add the pulp to the warm water. Soak for at least 4 hours.

2 Place a sieve (strainer) over a clean bowl. Pour the tamarind pulp and water into the sieve, then press the pulp through the sieve with the back of a wooden spoon, leaving the black seeds behind. Discard the seeds.

3 Add the sugar to the mixture and stir well until dissolved. Pour into a jug (pitcher) and chill thoroughly before serving in tumblers filled with ice.

Nutritional information per portion: Energy 61kcal/259kJ; Protein 0.4g; Carbohydrate 15.7g, of which sugars 15.7g; Fat 0g, of which saturates 0g; Cholesterol 0mg; Calcium 10mg; Fibre 0.5g; Sodium 2mg.

Sangrita

Sipping sangrita and tequila alternately is a taste sensation not to be missed, the warm flavours of the first balancing the harshness of the second.

SERVES 8

450g/1lb ripe tomatoes
1 small onion, finely chopped
2 small fresh green fresno chillies, seeded and chopped
120ml/4fl oz/¹/₂ cup juice from freshly squeezed oranges
juice of 3 limes
2.5ml/¹/₂ tsp caster (superfine) sugar
pinch of salt
1 small shot glass of golden or aged tequila per person

1 Cut a cross in the base of each tomato. Place the tomatoes in a heatproof bowl and pour over boiling water to cover. Leave for 3 minutes.

2 Lift the tomatoes out on a slotted spoon and plunge them into a second bowl of cold water. The skins will have begun to peel back from the crosses. Remove the skins, then cut the tomatoes in half and scoop out the seeds with a teaspoon.

3 Chop the tomato flesh and put in a food processor. Add the onion, chillies, orange juice, lime juice, sugar and salt.

4 Process until all the mixture is very smooth, then pour into a jug (pitcher) and chill for at least 1 hour before serving. Offer each drinker a separate shot glass of tequila as well. The drinks are sipped alternately.

Nutritional information per portion: Energy 72kcal/302kJ; Protein 0.5g; Carbohydrate 3.6g, of which sugars 3.4g; Fat 0.2g, of which saturates 0.1g; Cholesterol 0mg; Calcium 7mg; Fibre 0.6g; Sodium 6mg.

Sangria

Testament to the Spanish influence on Mexican cooking, this popular thirst-quencher is often served in large jugs, with ice and citrus fruit slices floating on top.

SERVES 6

750ml/1¹/₄ pints/3 cups dry red wine
juice of 2 limes
120ml/4fl oz/¹/₂ cup freshly squeezed orange juice
120ml/4fl oz/¹/₂ cup brandy
50g/2oz/¹/₄ cup caster (superfine) sugar
1 lime, sliced, to decorate
ice, to serve

1 Combine the wine, lime juice, orange juice and brandy in a large glass jug.

2 Stir in the sugar until it has dissolved completely.

3 Serve in tall glasses with ice. Decorate each glass with a slice of lime.

COOK'S TIP

If no caster sugar is available, use sugar syrup. Heat 50g/2oz/ ¹/₄ cup sugar in 50ml/2fl oz/¹/₄ cup water. Boil for 3 minutes, chill and store in a tightly sealed jar.

Nutritional information per portion: Energy 144kcal/602kJ; Protein 0.2g; Carbohydrate 10.4g, of which sugars 10.4g; Fat 0g, of which saturates 0g; Cholesterol 0mg; Calcium 13mg; Fibre 0g; Sodium 9mg.

Bloody Maria

A natural progression from Sangrita, this simple cocktail consists of tequila and tomato juice mixed together and served in the same glass.

SERVES 2

250ml/8fl oz/1 cup tomato juice, chilled
5ml/1 tsp Worcestershire sauce
60ml/4 tbsp tequila
few drops of Tabasco sauce
juice of 1/2 lemon
pinch of celery salt
salt and ground black pepper
**ice cubes and 2 celery sticks, cut into
    batons, to serve**

1 Pour the chilled tomato juice into a large jug and stir in the tequila. Add the Worcestershire sauce and stir the mixture well to combine the flavours.

2 Add a few drops of Tabasco sauce and the lemon juice. Taste and season with celery salt, salt and pepper. Serve over ice cubes, with celery batons.

Nutritional information per portion: Energy 82kcal/345kJ; Protein 0.9g; Carbohydrate 3.4g, of which sugars 3.4g; Fat 0g, of which saturates 0g; Cholesterol 0mg; Calcium 15mg; Fibre 0.6g; Sodium 260mg.

Strawberry and banana preparado

Similar to a smoothie, this is a thick, creamy fruit drink with an added kick that makes for a delicious cocktail. Leave out the alcohol if you prefer.

SERVES 4

200g/7oz/2 cups strawberries, hulled and chopped, plus extra to decorate
2 bananas, peeled and chopped
120ml/4fl oz/½ cup coconut cream
175ml/6fl oz/¾ cup white rum
60ml/4 tbsp grenadine
10 ice cubes

1 Put the fruit in a food processor or blender, and slowly add the coconut cream. Process until smooth, scraping down the sides of the goblet as necessary.

2 Add the rum, grenadine, and ice cubes, crushing the ice first unless you have a heavy-duty processor. Blend until smooth. Serve at once, decorated with extra strawberries.

Nutritional information per portion: Energy 211kcal/883kJ; Protein 1.5g; Carbohydrate 23.2g, of which sugars 22g; Fat 0.4g, of which saturates 0.1g; Cholesterol 0mg; Calcium 28mg; Fibre 1.7g; Sodium 41mg.

Café de olla

One of the most popular drinks in Mexico, this coffee is always drunk black. Traditionally the sweetener is piloncillo, *the local sugar, but any soft dark brown sugar can be used.*

SERVES 4

1 litre/1³/4 pints/4 cups water
115g/4oz/¹/2 cup *piloncillo* or soft dark brown sugar
4 cinnamon sticks, each about 15cm/6in long
50g/2oz/²/3 cup freshly ground coffee, from dark-roast
    coffee beans

1 Place the water, sugar and cinnamon sticks in a pan. Heat gently, stirring occasionally to make sure that the sugar dissolves, then bring to the boil. Boil rapidly for about 20 minutes until the syrup has reduced by a quarter.

2 Add the ground coffee to the syrup and stir well, then bring the liquid back to the boil. Remove from the heat, cover the pan and leave to stand for around 5 minutes.

3 Strain the coffee through a fine sieve, pour into cups and serve immediately.

Nutritional information per portion: Energy 99kcal/422kJ; Protein 0.2g; Carbohydrate 26.2g, of which sugars 26.1g; Fat 0g, of which saturates 0g; Cholesterol 0mg; Calcium 14mg; Fibre 0g; Sodium 2mg.

Atole

This drink has the consistency of a thick milkshake. Fresh fruit purées are often added before serving and some recipes introduce ground almonds or milk.

SERVES 6

200g/7oz/1³/4 cups white *masa harina*
1.2 litres/2 pints/5 cups water
1 vanilla pod
50g/2oz/¹/4 cup *piloncillo* or soft dark brown sugar
2.5ml/¹/2 tsp ground cinnamon
115g/4oz/1 cup fresh strawberries, chopped pineapple or orange
    segments (optional)

1 Put the *masa harina* in a heavy pan and gradually beat in the water to make a smooth paste.

2 Place the pan over a moderate heat add the vanilla pod and bring the mixture to the boil, stirring constantly until it thickens. Beat in the sugar and ground cinnamon and continue to beat until the sugar has dissolved. Remove from the heat.

3 If adding the fruit, purée it in a food processor or blender until smooth, then press the purée through a sieve.

4 Stir the purée into the mixture and return to the heat until warmed through. Remove the vanilla pod. Serve.

Nutritional information per portion: Energy 250kcal/1050kJ; Protein 4.8g; Carbohydrate 54g, of which sugars 17.4g; Fat 1.7g, of which saturates 0g; Cholesterol 0mg; Calcium 10mg; Fibre 1.1g; Sodium 1mg.

Café con leche

Many Mexicans start the day with this spiced milky coffee, and those who have enjoyed a hearty midday meal will often opt for a cup of it with a pastry as the afternoon merienda.

SERVES 4

50g/2oz/²⁄₃ cup ground coffee
475ml/16fl oz/2 cups boiling water
475ml/16fl oz/2 cups milk
4 cinnamon sticks, each about 10cm/4in long
sugar, to taste

1 Put the ground coffee in a cafetière (press pot) or jug (pitcher), pour on the boiling water and leave for a few minutes until the coffee grounds settle at the bottom.

2 Push down the plunger of the cafetière or strain the jug of coffee to separate the liquid from the grounds. Pour the strained coffee into a clean jug.

3 Pour the milk into a heavy pan, add the cinnamon sticks and bring to the boil, stirring occasionally.

4 Using a slotted spoon, lift out the cinnamon sticks and use a smaller spoon to press down on them to release any liquid they have absorbed. Set the cinnamon sticks aside for serving.

5 Add the coffee to the hot milk, then pour into cups. Add a cinnamon stick to each cup. Drinkers should add sugar to taste as required.

Nutritional information per portion: Energy 47kcal/198kJ; Protein 3.5g; Carbohydrate 4.8g, of which sugars 4.7g; Fat 1.7g, of which saturates 1.1g; Cholesterol 6mg; Calcium 121mg; Fibre 0g; Sodium 43mg.

Horchata

This aromatic rice drink is wonderfully creamy, yet does not contain any milk. Mexicans swear by it as a means of settling stomach upsets and it is often served at breakfast.

SERVES 4

450g/1lb/2¼ cups long grain rice
750ml/1¼ pints/3 cups water
150g/5oz/1¼ cups blanched whole almonds
10ml/2 tsp ground cinnamon
finely grated rind of 1 lime, plus strips of rind, to decorate
50g/2oz/¼ cup sugar
ice cubes, to serve

1 Tip the rice into a sieve and rinse thoroughly under cold running water. Drain, tip into a large bowl and pour over the water. Cover and soak for at least 2 hours, preferably overnight.

2 Drain the rice, reserving 600ml/1 pint/2½ cups of the soaking liquid. Spoon the rice into a food processor or blender and grind as finely as possible.

3 Add the almonds to the processor or blender and continue to grind in the same way until finely ground.

4 Add the cinnamon, grated lime rind and sugar to the ground rice and ground almonds. Add the reserved soaking water from the rice and mix until all the sugar has dissolved.

5 Serve in tall glasses with ice cubes. Decorate with strips of lime rind.

Nutritional information per portion: Energy 707kcal/2955kJ; Protein 16.3g; Carbohydrate 112g, of which sugars 21.2g; Fat 21.5g, of which saturates 1.7g; Cholesterol 0mg; Calcium 121mg; Fibre 2.8g; Sodium 7mg.

After-dinner coffee

A superb end to a meal. Kahlúa, the Mexican coffee liqueur used in this drink, is also delicious served in a liqueur glass and topped with a thin layer of cream.

SERVES 4

50g/2oz/¹/₃ cup dark-roast ground
   coffee
475ml/16fl oz/2 cups boiling water
120ml/4fl oz/¹/₂ cup tequila
120ml/4fl oz/¹/₂ cup Kahlúa liqueur
5ml/1 tsp natural vanilla extract
25g/1oz/2 tbsp soft dark brown sugar
150ml/¹/₄ pint/²/₃ cup double (heavy)
   cream

1 Put the ground coffee in a heatproof jug (pitcher) or cafetière (press pot), pour on the boiling water and leave until the coffee grounds settle.

2 Strain the jug of coffee through a sieve (strainer) or push down the plunger in the lid of the cafetière to separate the liquid from the grounds. Pour the strained coffee into a clean heatproof jug.

3 Add the tequila, Kahlúa and vanilla extract to the coffee and stir well to mix. Add the sugar and continue to stir until it has dissolved completely.

4 Pour the mixture into small coffee cups, liqueur coffee glasses or tall glasses that will withstand the heat of the coffee.

5 Hold a teaspoon just above the surface of one of the coffees. Pour the cream very slowly down the back of the spoon so that it forms a pool on top of the coffee. Repeat with the remaining coffees. Serve at once.

Nutritional information per portion: Energy 511kcal/2116kJ; Protein 1g; Carbohydrate 19g, of which sugars 19g; Fat 36.5g, of which saturates 19.5g; Cholesterol 80mg; Calcium 40mg; Fibre 0g; Sodium 43mg.

Rompope

Legend has it that this drink was first made in the kitchens of a convent in Puebla. It is traditional to seal bottles of Rompope with rolled corn husks or cobs which have been stripped of their corn.

**MAKES 1.5 LITRES/
2½ PINTS/6¼ CUPS**

1 litre/1¾ pints/4 cups milk
350g/12oz/1½ cups sugar
2.5ml/½ tsp bicarbonate of soda
1 cinnamon stick, about 15cm/6in long
12 large egg yolks
300ml/½ pint/1¼ cups dark rum

1 Pour the milk into a pan and stir in the sugar and bicarbonate of soda. Add the cinnamon stick. Place the pan over a moderate heat and bring the mixture to the boil, stirring constantly. Immediately pour the mixture into a bowl and cool to room temperature. Remove the cinnamon stick, squeezing it gently to release any liquid.

2 Put the egg yolks in a heatproof bowl over a pan of simmering water and whisk until the mixture is very thick and pale.

3 Add the yolks to the milk a little at a time, beating after each addition. Return the mixture to a clean pan, place over a low heat and cook until it thickens and the back of the spoon is visible when a finger is drawn along it.

4 Stir in the rum, pour into sterilized bottles and seal tightly with stoppers or clear film (plastic wrap). Chill until required. Serve *rompope* very cold. It will keep for up to 1 week in the fridge.

Nutritional information per portion: Energy 397kcal/1666kJ; Protein 10.5g; Carbohydrate 38.5g, of which sugars 38.5g; Fat 13.3g, of which saturates 4.6g; Cholesterol 411mg; Calcium 223mg; Fibre 0g; Sodium 77mg.

Champurrada

This popular version of atole *is made with Mexican chocolate. A special wooden whisk called a* molinollo *is traditionally used when making this frothy drink.*

SERVES 6

115g/4oz Mexican chocolate, about 2 discs
1.2 litres/2 pints/5 cups water or milk, or a mixture
200g/7oz white *masa harina*
30ml/2 tbsp soft dark brown sugar

1 Put the chocolate in a mortar and grind with a pestle until it becomes a fine powder. Alternatively, grind the chocolate in a food processor.

2 Put the liquid in a heavy pan and gradually stir in all the *masa harina* until a smooth paste is formed. Use a traditional wooden *molinollo*, if you have one, or a wire whisk for a frothier drink.

3 Place the pan over a moderate heat and bring the mixture to the boil, stirring all the time until the frothy drink thickens.

4 Stir in the ground chocolate, then add the sugar. Serve immediately.

Nutritional information per portion: Energy 250kcal/1048kJ; Protein 6g; Carbohydrate 41.6g, of which sugars 18.8g; Fat 6.8g, of which saturates 3.5g; Cholesterol 5mg; Calcium 89mg; Fibre 1.1g; Sodium 30mg.

Mexican hot chocolate

Mexican chocolate is flavoured with almonds, cinnamon and vanilla, and is sweetened with sugar. Making the chocolate is fiddly, but fortunately the discs can be bought in stores.

SERVES 4

1 litre/1¾ pints/4 cups milk
50–115g/2–4oz Mexican chocolate (1–2 discs)
1 vanilla pod

1 Pour the milk into a small pan and add the chocolate discs. Precisely how much to use will depend on your personal taste. Start with one disc and use more the next time if necessary.

2 Split the vanilla pod lengthways using a sharp knife, and add it to the milk.

3 Heat the chocolate milk gently, stirring until all the chocolate has dissolved, then whisking with a wire whisk or a *molinollo* until the mixture boils. Remove the vanilla pod and divide the drink among four mugs or heatproof glasses. Serve at once.

Nutritional information per portion: Energy 220kcal/924kJ; Protein 8.1g; Carbohydrate 25.3g, of which sugars 25.1g; Fat 10.4g, of which saturates 6.4g; Cholesterol 13mg; Calcium 248mg; Fibre 0.6g; Sodium 88mg.

The Mexican kitchen

This section looks at the development

of regional Mexican cuisine and provides

an essential guide to all the ingredients

used in Mexican cooking, such as rice,

chocolate, herbs and spices. It also gives

lots of helpful information on preparation,

equipment and cooking techniques.

Regional cooking

Mexico has not one single cuisine, but many. It is a vast country, the third largest in Latin America, with a wide diversity of landscapes, from snow-capped mountains to citrus groves, and a distinct range of climatic zones. These geographical factors have helped to shape a variety of different styles of cooking within the same country.

The altitude, rather than the latitude, determines the climate in Mexico and the produce each area grows is different. The coastal region below 914m/3000ft is *tierra caliente* – the hot zone. Here the climate is sub-tropical, and mangoes, pineapples and avocados flourish. Next comes *tierra templada*, the temperate zone, which rises to 1800m/6000ft. Many familiar vegetables and fruits are grown in Mexico, including green beans, peppers, tomatoes, cabbages, cauliflowers, onions, aubergines and courgettes. At the greatest altitude lies the cold zone (*tierra fria*).

THE NORTH

The northern area of Mexico, stretching from Sonora, near the Gulf of California, to Monterrey in Nuevo León, has some striking contrasts. Sonora and Chihuahua are the cattle rearing parts of the country. Good grazing encouraged the Spanish to establish herds of their hardy longhorns here, and specialities of the region include a beef stew called *caldiddo* and the famous dried beef, or *carne seca*. This is produced by

BELOW: *Fruit and vegetables for sale at a market in San Christobal de las Casas.*

first salting the beef, then drying it and finally treating it with lemon juice and pepper.

Monterrey is the industrial heart of the region. Brewing employs a large percentage of the population, and this is the home of *frijoles borrachos* (drunken beans), a dish that consists of beans cooked in beer with onion, spices and garlic. The north of Mexico is also the main cheese-producing region. Chihuahua is known for a dish called *chiles con queso* – melted cheese with chilli strips.

The greatest treasure of the north is the soft flour tortilla, produced here because this is the only part of Mexico where wheat is grown. *Burritos*, portable parcels of meat, beans and rice wrapped in wheat flour tortillas, are typical of this region.

THE COASTAL REGIONS

The northern Pacific coast has some magnificent beaches. The sea is well stocked with fish, especially bass, tuna and swordfish. *Ceviche*, that delicious dish made of raw fish "cooked" by the action of lime juice, is very popular. This area has good soil, and grains of various types are widely cultivated, as well as chillies and other vegetables.

Further south is the state of Jalisco, the home of tequila. Inland is the colonial town of Guadalajara, famous for *pozole*, a centuries-old recipe for pork stew. The cuisine of this area – Oaxaca – has strong Spanish influences, but is also home to some very traditional Mexican dishes, such as the *moles* – rich meat stews that incorporate nuts and chocolate.

ABOVE: *Baskets of dried chillies and other fruit for sale on the streets of Mexico City.*

The eastern seaboard is known as the Gulf Coast. The climate is tropical, and this is reflected in the food. Bananas, vanilla, avocados, coffee and coconuts grow on the coast, mangoes and pineapples in the south, and to the north are apples and pears.

The Gulf Coast has abundant fish stocks. The southern state of Tabasco, on the isthmus of Tehuantepec, is particularly famous for its fish.

THE BAJIO, CENTRAL MEXICO AND MEXICO CITY

North of Mexico City is the Bajio, a fertile area bordered by mountains, sometimes referred to as Colonial Mexico. Many of the local specialities are distinctly Spanish in origin, such as stuffed tongues and beef stews.

There are traditional Mexican foods here too, especially *nopales* (cactus paddles) and prickly pears (cactus fruit). *Pulque* – a drink made from the juice of the agave plant – is popular in this area. Pork is the favourite meat, often served as *carnitas*.

Central Mexico, a land-locked area, lies to the south of Mexico City, and includes the towns of Puebla and Tlaxcala. Puebla is associated with the dish *mole poblano*.

THE SOUTH

In the Yucatán, the poor soil does not readily support agriculture, but corn is grown in areas where the vegetation has been cut and burned, and is ground to make meal, *masa harina*, used for corn tortillas. Good fish, squid and shellfish, including large prawns, are available all along the coast. *Huevos motuleños*, a dish of eggs with refried beans and tomato sauce, is a well known Yucatec dish.

Equipment

You need very little by way of specialist equipment in order to cook Mexican food. Most modern Mexican kitchens today have a food processor to do much of the chopping and grinding. However, the items listed below will make many of the tasks easier and are worth investing in if you make a lot of Mexican food.

TORTILLA PRESS

Traditionally, tortillas were always shaped by hand. Skilled women were able to make an astonishing number of perfectly shaped tortillas in a very short time, but this is something of a dying art today. Most people now use metal tortilla presses. Cast iron presses are the most effective, but they must be seasoned (oiled) before use and well cared for, so many people today prefer steel presses. These come in various sizes and are

heavy, in order to limit the leverage required to work them. Cover the plates with plastic bags or waxed paper and it will be easier to lift the tortillas once they are pressed. Tortilla presses are available in good specialist kitchenware shops and by mail order.

COMAL

This is a thin, circular griddle, traditionally used over an open fire to cook tortillas. A cast iron griddle or large frying pan will do this job equally well.

METATE

A *metate* is a grinding stone used to grind corn to make masa. It is also used to grind cocoa and *piloncillo* (unrefined cane sugar). The design has not changed for centuries. Made from a sloping piece of volcanic rock, it has three short legs. Before a new *metate* can be used, it must be tempered. A mixture of dry rice and salt is placed on the grinding surface and the *muller* – the implement that does the actual grinding – is used to press the mixture into the surface and remove any loose pieces of sand or grit. The *muller* is

ABOVE: *A metate is a grinding stone used for grinding corn, sugar and cocoa.*

made of the same stone as the *metate* and is called a *mano* or *metlapil*. These are quite difficult to locate outside Mexico, but are available by mail order.

Tortilla warmer

Ideal for keeping tortillas warm at the table, this is a small round basket or clay dish with a lid. The size that is most readily available outside Mexico is suitable for 15cm/6in tortillas. Look for them in specialist kitchenware shops.

Tortilla press

Comal

MOLINOLLO

A carved wooden implement used for whisking drinking chocolate. Some of these are beautiful and are popular with tourists. A wire whisk can also be used.

OLLAS

These are the clay pots traditionally used for cooking stews and sauces. They give food a unique flavour, but are seldom to be found outside Mexico, as they are becoming relatively rare in Mexico too. Flat earthenware dishes decorated around the edge are used for serving and are more easily found than *ollas*.

MOLCAJETE AND TEJOLOTE

The mortar and pestle of Mexico, the *molcajete* and *tejolote* are made from porous volcanic rock and must be tempered in the same way as the *metate* before being used. They are ideal for grinding spices such as achiote (annatto) or for grinding nuts and seeds when making *mole poblano*.

Molinollo and wire whisk

Patterned ceramic dishes

Molcajete and tejolote

Ollas

Corn

The native Indians of Mexico regarded corn as a gift from the gods. How otherwise would they have come by such a versatile food, which is so hardy and adaptable and able to flourish in all the different climates and soils of their country?

White corn

The native Indians offered up gifts to the god of corn, celebrated him on feast days and even added tiny grains of corn pollen to their traditional sand paintings to give the artworks healing powers. A popular myth held that corn was in fact the very stuff from which the gods created people. Even now, corn accounts for 20 per cent of the world's food calories.

In the traditional Navajo wedding ceremony, the bride's grandmother presents the couple with a basket of cornmeal and the couple exchange a handful with each other – such is the significance of corn in their culture.

Every part of the corn cob is used in Mexican culture: the husks for wrapping *tamales*, the silk in medicines, the kernels for food and the stalks for animal feed. The husks from corn cobs are most commonly used for *tamales*, but they are also used for wrapping some other foods

before cooking. When they are ready, the husks will peel away from the filling. The husks are not eaten, but are discarded once the *tamales* are cooked. In Oaxaca, *tamales* are wrapped in banana leaves rather than corn husks, which impart a distinctly different flavour.

Preparing dried corn husks
If you are able to buy dried corn husks you will need to make them soft and pliable before using.

1 Soak the corn husks in a bowl of cold water for several hours. When they are soft, remove them from the bowl and pat dry.

2 Place the husks flat on a dry surface. Pile the filling on the centre of the husk and fold into neat parcels. Tie to secure them before steaming.

Dried corn husks

Fresh corn husks

VARIETIES AND USES

Corn is the common name for a cereal grass. With wheat and rice, it is one of the world's key grain crops. A native of the Americas, it was introduced into Europe by Columbus, who brought it to Spain. A wide variety of products are produced from corn, including corn syrup, bourbon and starch. There are a few main types of corn used for food, each with several different varieties.

Flint corn This is also known as Indian corn and is described as "flint" because of the hard texture of the kernel. This can be red, blue, brown or purple, which has made this type of corn a popular choice for some of the more novel foods such as blue or red corn tortilla chips. Popcorn is made from a type of flint corn. Predominantly, however, flint corn is used for industrial purposes and animal feed.

Yellow corn A type of "dent" corn, so called because the sides of the kernel are composed of a hard starch and the crown of a softer starch which shrinks to form the characteristic depression or dent.

Yellow corn has large, full-flavoured kernels and is used for making many processed foods. It is also the basic ingredient used in corn syrup, cornstarch and corn oil.

White corn is used to make masa, a type of dough that is widely used in Mexican cooking.

Flour corn is composed largely of soft starch and can be ground to make flour for use in baked products. Grinding produces the very white cornflour with which we are familiar, and which is the main constituent of custard powder.

Sweetcorn contains more natural sugar than other types of corn. The kernels can be eaten straight from the cooked cob and in Mexico a favourite snack is elotes con crema, where the corn cobs are dipped in cream and sprinkled with fresh cheese before being served. The kernels can also be stripped from the cobs and used in soups and vegetable dishes. As soon as the cob is picked, the sugar in the kernels starts to convert to starch. This reduces the natural sweetness, so it is important that the corn is eaten as soon as possible after being picked.

MASA/MASA HARINA

Masa is the Mexican word for dough, and specifically refers to the fresh corn dough used to make corn tortillas and other corn dishes. The flour – or masa harina – is traditionally made with sun-dried or fire-dried white corn kernels that have been cooked in water mixed with lime (calcium oxide, not the fruit). They are then soaked in the lime water overnight. The lime helps to swell the kernels and bring about a chemical change which improves the flavour of the masa. The wet corn is ground, using a metate – a traditional grinding stone which no self-respecting Mexican kitchen would be without. The resulting masa can be used for making corn tortillas – for tamales, other ingredients need to be added, such as chicken stock and lard.

Two types of masa harina

Red corn

Blue corn

Tortillas

Mexican tortillas are a type of flat, unleavened bread made from either finely ground corn or wheat flour. It is very easy to make your own, but if you are short of time, they are readily available in supermarkets.

CORN TORTILLAS

Have ready a tortilla press and two clean plastic bags, slit if necessary so that they will lie flat. If you don't have a press, you can use a rolling pin instead. It is traditional to cook tortillas on a special griddle called a *comal*, but a cast iron griddle or large heavy frying pan will work just as well.

ABOVE: *Wheat flour tortillas (left) are more common in the north of Mexico and used to make* burritos *and* fajitas. *Corn tortillas (right) are perfect for making* tacos, toastadas *and* enchiladas. *They can be bough from supermarkets.*

How to make corn tortillas

MAKES 12 X 15CM/6IN TORTILLAS

275g/10oz/2 cups *masa harina*
pinch of salt
250ml/8fl oz/1 cup warm water

1 Place the *masa harina*, salt and warm water in a large bowl. Mix together until it forms a dough.

2 Turn out the dough on to a lightly floured surface and knead well for 3–4 minutes until firm, smooth and no longer sticky. Cover with clear film (plastic wrap) and leave the dough to stand at room temperature for 1 hour.

3 Pinch off 12 pieces of dough of equal size and, using your fingers, roll each piece of dough into a ball. Work with one piece of dough at a time, keeping the rest covered with clear film or a dishtowel to stop drying out.

4 Open the tortilla press and place a plastic bag on the base. Put a dough ball on top and then press with the palm of your hand to flatten slightly.

5 Lay a second plastic bag on top of the round of dough and close the press. Press down firmly several times to flatten the dough into a thin round.

6 Heat a frying pan or griddle. Remove the tortilla from the press and remove the plastic bags.

7 Flip the tortilla on to the hot frying pan or griddle and cook for about 1 minute over medium heat, or until the lower surface is blistered and is just beginning to turn golden brown. Turn the tortilla over using a palette knife and cook the other side for a further minute. Cook the remaining tortillas in the same way. Meanwhile, keep the cooked tortillas warm by wrapping them in a clean, dry dishtowel until you are ready to serve them.

FLOUR TORTILLAS

Wheat flour tortillas are more common than corn tortillas in the north of Mexico. For best results, make sure you use a good plain (all-purpose) flour.

How to make flour tortillas

MAKES ABOUT 12 X 25CM/10 IN TORTILLAS

500g/1¼ lb/5 cups plain (all-purpose) flour, sifted
2.5ml/½ tsp baking powder
pinch of salt
100g/3¾ oz/scant ½ cup lard
about 120ml/4fl oz/½ cup warm water

1 Mix the flour, baking powder and salt in a bowl. Rub in the lard, then gradually add warm water to draw the flour together into a stiff dough.

2 Turn out the dough on to a lightly floured work surface and knead it for 10–15 minutes until it is elastic. Divide the dough into 12 even-size pieces and roll into balls using the palms of your hand. Cover while you are working to stop them drying out.

Folding and cooking tortillas

Many Mexican dishes are made with tortillas. The difference in the name lies in the filling, folding and cooking.

3 Roll out each ball on a lightly floured surface. Give the dough a quarter turn after each roll to keep the round even. Keep rolling until the round is about 30cm/12in.

4 Warm a cast-iron griddle or a large heavy frying pan over a medium heat. Cook one tortilla at a time, placing each one in the ungreased pan or on the griddle and cooking it for 45 seconds to 1 minute, or until the lower surface begins to blister and brown. Turn the tortilla over and cook the other side for about 1 minute. Wrap the cooked tortillas in a clean, dry dishtowel to keep them soft and warm while you make the rest.

COOK'S TIP

To reheat cold tortillas, sprinkle them with a few drops of water, wrap them in foil and place in an oven preheated to 140°C/275°F/Gas 1 for 10 minutes.

Burritos These are flour tortilla envelopes enclosing various fillings and then folded into the classic shape and the edges sealed with flour and water.

Chimichangas A chimichanga is a burrito that has been folded, chilled to allow the edges to seal and then deep fried in hot oil until crisp and golden.

Enchiladas These can be made from either corn or wheat tortillas. A little filling is laid down the centre of a tortilla, which is then rolled to make a tube, rather like cannelloni. Filled tortillas are laid side by side in a baking dish before being topped with a sauce and baked in the oven or finished under the grill.

Fajitas These are ideal for informal dinner parties, as various fillings are placed on the table with the hot tortillas, and guests fill and roll their own.

Quesadillas These treats are made by placing a corn or flour tortilla in a warm frying pan and spreading one half lightly with salsa. A little chicken or a few prawns (shrimp) are sometimes added, and fresh cheese is sprinkled on top. The other half of the tortilla is then folded over, and the quesadilla is cooked for 1–2 minutes, during which time it is turned once.

Tacos True Mexican tacos are corn tortillas that have been filled and folded in half; they still remain soft.

Tostadas These are individual corn tortillas which are fried until they are crisp and then topped with shredded meat, refried beans, salsa, guacamole, sour cream and a little fresh cheese. The finger-food versions are called *tostaditas*.

Rice and beans

Rice was first introduced to Mexico by the Spanish and is now a staple ingredient of Mexican cooking. But the importance of beans in the Mexican diet really cannot be overestimated. Indigenous to the country, they were cultivated by the Indians along with corn, and the two staple crops coexisted. Successive plantings of corn soon deplete the soil; beans enrich it by introducing nitrogen. The early inhabitants knew this, and planted them together.

RICE

Mexicans have been using rice since it was introduced to the country by the Spanish in the 16th century. It was originally brought to the town of Acapulco in Mexico from the Philippines in the famous ship *Nao de China* and was also shipped on to Spain itself.

The Spaniards later found the lush tropical climate of the Veracruz region of Mexico to be a perfect growing ground for rice. From there it grew to culinary prominence.

The rice grown and used in Mexico is long grain – this means that each grain is four times longer than its width. White long grain rice which has had the husk removed, is the most common type available in Mexico, although it is often not as refined as the white rice most widely sold in the West.

Most rice for sale in the West comes in packets. It keeps extremely well in a cool, dry place, but once packages are opened, any unused rice should be transferred to an airtight container. For Mexican food, it is important to use a rice that absorbs the flavours of other ingredients well.

Rice is traditionally served as the second course of the midday meal. It may be served turned out of a mould to be eaten with beans or with fish. However, the classic Mexican dish of rice and beans is actually not at all typical of Mexican cooking.

Cooking tips

Rice is used in a variety of Mexican dishes, from *sopa seca* (dry soup), which is served as a separate course in the *comida* or main meal, to rice pudding. When served as an accompaniment, rice is usually mixed with other ingredients, as in the popular green rice, which includes chillies, and yellow rice, which owes its colour to *achiote* (annatto). Ground rice is used as a flour (*harina de arroz*) in cakes or biscuits. Most Mexicans tend to soak their rice in boiled water for a minimum of 10 minutes before they cook it. This reduces the cooking time and also encourages the rice to absorb other flavours. After soaking, it should be rinsed repeatedly and drained thoroughly before being cooked.

Long grain rice

Ground rice

BEANS

Beans continue to be a staple food in Mexico, and there will be a pot of dried beans simmering daily on the cooker top in every home. Fresh beans are eaten, too, of course, but it is the dried beans, with their better keeping properties, that are most widely used. With their shiny and speckled skins, they make a colourful display on market stalls and there are many different varieties to choose from.

Popular varieties

Pinto beans and black beans are the most commonly used dried beans in Mexico, although butter (lima) beans, which are sold both fresh and dried, are used in a number of dishes and side dishes.

Chickpeas In Mexico, these are called *garbanzos*. They are not native to the country, but were brought in from the Middle East. They have become popular, however, and feature in several dishes.

Pinto beans Pinto is Spanish for "painted" and refers to the speckles of red-brown on the pale pink skins. A rich source of protein and iron, they are only available dried. Mexicans use them for all sorts of dishes, but it is as *frijoles de olla*, the simple bean dish that is eaten daily in most homes, that they are most familiar. The cooked beans are the basis of *refritos* (refried beans), and are used in salsas.

Black beans Small, with black skins and cream-coloured flesh, these beans have a wonderfully sweet flavour. Do not confuse them with black-eyed beans, which are white, with a black eye. Black beans are used in soups and salsas, and can be substituted for pinto beans in *frijoles de olla*.

Cooking tips

To cook pre-soaked dried beans, simply drain them thoroughly, then put them in a clean pan with plenty of water. Do not add salt, as this would cause the skins on the beans to toughen. Bring the water to the boil and then cook for the time recommended in the individual recipes, usually 1–1¼ hours. Cooking times can vary considerably, so always taste for tenderness before finally draining and serving the beans.

Preparation

Before you use dried beans, put them in a colander or sieve and pick them over, removing any foreign bodies, then rinse them thoroughly under cold running water. Drain, tip into a large bowl and pour over plenty of cold water.

Pinto beans

Black beans

Chickpeas

Chocolate, nuts and seeds

Sweets, puddings, cakes and pastries are much loved by the Mexicans, but the sweet ingredients that go into these are also used in savoury dishes, and chocolate, along with various types of nuts and seeds, is a very important element of Mexican cooking.

CHOCOLATE

When the Spanish reached Mexico, they discovered a wealth of unfamiliar ingredients, including potatoes, vanilla, avocados and squash. One of their greatest finds,

however, was chocolate. The Aztecs were very partial to a drink made from the beans of the cacao tree, which they flavoured in many different ways, and the Spanish, like the rest of the world after them, embraced this wonderful new taste with enthusiasm, developing a fondness for a variation that included corn, honey and spices.

The conquistadors took chocolate back to Spain, and it was not long before all the most fashionable resorts and cities in Europe boasted cocoa houses. Initially it was served as a drink, but Spanish women also prepared it as a sweetmeat, mixing it with sugar, cinnamon, eggs and almonds. Europeans started producing chocolate in slabs some two hundred years later. When slabs of chocolate were finally produced in Mexico, the chocolate was sweetened and spiced in Spanish style.

Mexican chocolate

This is produced using dark and bitter chocolate mixed with sugar, ground nuts and cinnamon, and then pressed into discs. The chocolate has a grainy quality, thanks to the sugar and almonds, and it is quite crumbly when broken. One of the most popular brands is *Ibarra*. Some specialist suppliers outside Mexico stock this product. Check the packet for a use-by date and store in a cool, dry place.

LEFT: *Discs of* Ibarra *chocolate come in a distinctive yellow hexagonal box.*

Using chocolate to make beverages

The main use for chocolate in Mexico is still as a beverage. Mexicans are very partial to *Champurrada*, a chocolate corn drink, and the classic Mexican hot chocolate, which is whisked to a froth with a special whisk called a *molinollo*. Mexican hot chocolate is served with *churros*, long fritters which are dunked in the drink, or *pan dulce*, the sweet bread that Mexicans eat for breakfast.

The extra ingredients make Mexican chocolate unsuitable for *moles*, the rich stews to which chocolate is traditionally added, so bitter chocolate or cocoa is used. If you cannot buy Mexican chocolate, you can make an acceptable substitute using dark bitter chocolate and adding the sugar and spices yourself.

NUTS AND SEEDS

The three types of nut that are most widely used in Mexican cooking are the pecan, walnut and almond. Pine nuts are used in some desserts and pastries, and coconuts are valued both for their flesh and the cooling liquid they contain. Pecans grow in Northern Mexico and walnuts, which were introduced from Europe, are cultivated in the colder, central highlands.

The Spanish introduced almonds into Mexican cooking during the colonial era, but ensured that the trade with Spain was not disrupted by making it illegal for Mexicans themselves to cultivate them on a large scale. Seeds from pumpkin and squash have been important ingredients in Mexican cooking for centuries. At one time, pumpkins were grown mainly for their seeds and the flesh was discarded. Sesame seeds are also used, both in pastes and as a garnish.

Main uses of nuts and seeds

Salted or coated with sugar, pecans are eaten as a snack food, but their primary use is in desserts such as pecan cake. Almonds are used extensively, either whole, chopped or ground, in sweet and savoury dishes, including soups. Mexicans use ground almonds to thicken sauces, and substitute ground almonds for flour in some cakes and biscuits. Walnuts are also used in biscuits and cakes, including *polvorones de nuez*, which are traditionally eaten around Christmas time (Christmas cookies with walnuts).

Roasted salted pumpkin seeds are often served as snacks, while ground pumpkin seeds are used in sauces such as *pepián* (pumpkin seed sauce). Pine nuts, known as *piñon* seeds in Mexico, are added to dishes like *picadillo* and are also ground for use in desserts and cakes.

Cooking tips

When dry roasting or toasting pumpkin or sesame seeds, watch them carefully so that they do not burn. Use a heavy pan placed over a low heat, and stir or shake the pan frequently to keep the seeds on the move at all times. If they are allowed to burn, they will taste bitter and spoil the flavour of any dish to which they are added.

Pumpkin seeds

Sesame seeds

Pine nuts

Pecans, almonds and walnuts

Fruit

Visit any Mexican market and what will strike you first are the colourful displays of fruit of every size, shape and colour, such as mangoes, papayas, guavas, pineapples, and limes.

CITRUS FRUITS

All types of citrus fruit grow well in Mexico, and because the fruit is allowed to ripen naturally on the trees, it tends to have a very good flavour.

Limes have very thin skins which would eventually turn yellow if they were left on the tree long enough. The pulp of this fruit is green and juicy. Mexican limes – *limones* – are smaller than other varieties. Lemons are more of an oval shape, and have thicker skins. Oranges grow well in Mexico and freshly squeezed orange juice is widely available, especially in the south of the country.

Uses and cooking tips

Limes, lemons and oranges are used extensively in Mexican cooking, in both savoury and sweet dishes. The most famous use of limes – other than with tequila – is in *ceviche*. Raw fish or shellfish is marinated in the lime juice until the texture of the flesh becomes firm and white. Citrus juices are also used to prevent vegetables or fruits, such as avocados and bananas, from discolouring on contact with the air.

The rind on citrus fruits is often thinly pared or grated and used for decoration or flavouring, particularly in Mexican desserts. The skins of oranges are often ground, and the oil is used as a flavouring.

GUAVAS

These fruits are native to the tropical areas of South America. Guavas vary in colour, shape and size. The variety most popular in Mexico is the yellow guava. The skin is thick and inside is a creamy pulp, which is full of seeds.

Uses and cooking tips

Guavas are usually used in desserts, as part of a fruit platter for example, but their flavour is such that they are equally good in savoury dishes and also go very well with cheese.

To prepare, cut the fruit in half and scrape out the flesh with a spoon. The seeds can be eaten, or the pulp can be pressed through a sieve if preferred.

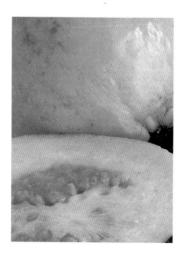

ABOVE: *Guavas are either served on their own or as an accompaniment to soft cheese.*

The flesh of guavas can also be used to make a delicious jelly or jam.

GRANADILLAS

These fruits are the largest members of the passion fruit family. Native to South America, they are round, with a small stalk attached at one end. The tough, shell-like outer skin is bright orange, while the pulp inside is green and very seedy.

Uses and cooking tips

Granadilla pulp can be used in desserts, either with the seeds, or sieved. It is often poured over ice cream or fruit salad, either on its own or in a dessert sauce. It also makes a superb fruit drink and the sieved pulp is often mixed with fresh orange juice. Cut the fruit in half and scoop out the pulp with a teaspoon. The seeds are edible, but sieve the pulp if you prefer.

ABOVE: *Granadillas are native to South America and the pulp is used in desserts.*

ABOVE: *Mangoes are either eaten on their own or used in a range of desserts.*

ABOVE: *Firm prickly pears will ripen if left for a few days at room temperature.*

ABOVE: *Pineapples must be picked ripe so the starch doesn't convert into sugar.*

MANGOES

Perhaps the most popular of all tropical fruits, magoes have a wonderful perfume when ripe. There are thousands of varieties of mango. All magoes start off green but most will change to yellow, golden or red when they are ripe.

Uses and cooking tips

It has been said that the best way to eat a mango is in the bath, because they are so juicy. Failing that, use a sharp knife to take a lengthways slice off either side of the fruit, as close to the stone as possible. Scoop out the mango flesh from each slice, then cut the rest of the flesh off the stone to make sure that none is wasted.

Mexicans eat mangoes just as they are, but also use them to good effect in a range of delicious desserts and drinks, such as mango and paech margarita, whereby the classic tequila recipe is given a fruity twist.

PRICKLY PEARS

Prickly pears are the fruits of several different types of cactus. Popular all over South America, prickly pears also serve as a staple food in some of the poorer rural areas of Mexico.

Uses and cooking tips

The fleshy leaves of prickly pears – *nopales* – are edible and are treated as a vegetable.

The prickles on prickly pears are usually removed before they are sold, but if not, they can be scrubbed off with a stiff brush before the fruit is peeled. It is essential to wear kitchen gloves to protect your hands while doing this.

To prepare, the peeled fruit should be halved and the flesh scooped out with a teaspoon. It can be strained and used as a sauce, or the fruit can be served as part of a fruit platter. The flesh of prickly pears can also be made into a delicious jelly or jam.

PINEAPPLES

Pineapples originated in South America and were introduced to other tropical areas by the Spanish and Portuguese. Although most ripe pineapples are yellow or orange, some varieties, such as the Sugar Loaf pineapple that is grown in Mexico, are green when fully ripe. Pineapple flesh is yellow and very juicy, with a sweet flavour that can be tangy or even slightly tart.

Uses and cooking tips

Mexican pineapples are deliciously sweet, and are usually served quite simply, as dessert. Pineapple is often combined with rice, in savoury dishes as well as sweet, and is used in puddings and sweetmeats. Pineapple juice is very popular, and is widely used in *agua fresca* sold by street vendors. When buying a pineapple, choose one that is slightly soft to the touch and which has a strong flavour.

Fruit vegetables

There are some fruits that are used so often in savoury dishes that we tend to think of them as vegetables. Tomatoes are the obvious example, but avocados, peppers and chillies also come into this category. Mexico also has the tomatillo, which is closely related to the cape gooseberry.

AVOCADOS

It is believed that the Aztecs introduced avocado seedlings to Mexico during the 13th and 14th centuries, calling them *ahuacatl*, a name whose Spanish version was first corrupted to alligator pear and then to the name avocado.

There are several varieties of avocado. Most are pear-shaped and contain a central stone. The flesh ranges in colour from creamy yellow through to bright green and has a buttery texture and mild but distinctive flavour.

Uses and cooking tips

Avocados are used extensively in Mexican cookery, most famously in guacamole, the mashed avocado dip. They are also used in soups.

TOMATOES

Tomatoes are native to western South America and were cultivated by the Aztecs long before the Spanish

ABOVE: *Tomatillos are often used in fresh and cooked Mexican sauce recipes. The presence of the distinctive papery husk indicates freshness.*

invasion. Hernán Cortés is credited with introducing the first tomatoes – yellow ones – to Europe. They were initially treated with suspicion, but after a pair of Jesuit priests introduced red tomatoes to Italy in the 18th century, they became more popular.

There are numerous varieties of tomato, ranging from tiny cherry tomatoes to ridged beefsteak tomatoes that measure as much as 10cm/4in across.

Uses and cooking tips

Mexicans use tomatoes in so many of their recipes that it would be impossible to list them all. They feature in hot and cold soups, salsas, salads as well as meat and fish dishes.

If a recipe requires that a tomato be seeded, cut it in half and squeeze gently, or scoop out the seeds with a teaspoon. To peel off the skin, cut a cross in the base of the tomato, immerse it in boiling water for 3 minutes, then plunge it into a bowl of cold water. Drain well. The skins will then be easy to remove.

TOMATILLOS/TOMATE VERDE

Tomatillos are not members of the tomato family, but are related to physalis, those pretty little orange fruit surrounded by papery lanterns. They have been grown in Mexico since Aztec times, when they were known as *miltomatl*.

Ranging in colour from yellowish green to lime, depending on their ripeness, tomatillos are firm, round fruit, about the size of a small tomato, but not as juicy. Fresh tomatillos usually still have the brown papery husk attached to them at the stem end. The flavour resembles that of tart apples with a hint of lemon, and is enhanced by cooking.

Main uses

Tomatillos are used in table salsas such as pinto bean salsa and in green tomatillo sauce (*tomate verde salsa*), which is poured over enchiladas before they are cooked.

PLANTAINS

Although native to Southeast Asia, plantains are popular in many Latin American countries, and particularly in those that have a coastline on the Caribbean sea.

Plantains are a type of banana, although they are larger than the sweet bananas and with a harder skin. The plantain flesh is fibrous and starchy and must be cooked before being eaten.

Uses and cooking tips

Plantains are used in both sweet and savoury dishes. Fried plantain slices are delicious with a chilli dip. Slices can be cooked in butter and served as a vegetable. They make a delectable dessert. Just cook them in butter and cinnamon, with a little sugar and a good measure of rum.

Plantains can't simply be unzipped, like bananas. Removing the flesh can be quite tricky, unless they are really ripe. The best way to remove the flesh is to cut the plantains into short lengths, then slit the skin along one of the natural ridges so that it can be carefully eased apart and removed. Unless you are going to use the peeled plantains immediately, put them in a bowl of acidulated water (water to which lime or lemon juice has been added) to prevent them from discolouring on contact with the air.

PEPPERS

Sometimes known as bell peppers or capsicums, these are native to Mexico and Central America, and were also a staple food for the Incas in Peru. They range in colour from green through yellow and orange to deep red, and there is even a purplish-black variety. They have a mild, sweet flavour and crisp, juicy flesh.

LEFT: *Green plantains are unripe, while yellow plantains are half-ripe.*

Uses and cooking tips

Peppers are used extensively in Mexican cuisine, contributing colour and flavour to salsas and stews, as well as fish and vegetable dishes.

Inside each pepper is a core that is surrounded by seeds, which must be removed. If the peppers are to be used whole, this can be lifted out if a neat slice is taken off the top, around the stem. If the peppers are halved or quartered, removing the core and seeds is even easier. Many recipes call for peppers to be roasted over a gas flame or in a dry frying pan, then sealed in a plastic bag until the steam loosens the skin, which is removed before the peppers are chopped.

NOPALES

Nopales are the edible leaves of several varieties of prickly pear cactus. Fat and fleshy, they are often called cactus paddles. Mexicans have been cooking and eating them for thousands of years. The leaves are oval in shape, with sharp spines. The flavour is similar to that of a green bean, but with a slightly acidic tang.

Uses and cooking tips

Nopales are used in stews and soups, particularly in the Tlaxcala area of Mexico, and are pickled for use in salsas and salad dishes. They are even added to scrambled eggs.

LEFT: *Red, yellow, green and orange peppers add colour to many dishes.*

Chillies

Chillies have been grown in South America for thousands of years. Over 150 indigenous varieties are found in Mexico alone. In 1492 Columbus brought chillies back with him to Europe and since then they have become staples of cuisines all over the world.

Mexican food is often perceived as being very hot, and some of the dishes certainly live up to their reputation, but it is possible to find many dishes that are only mildly flavoured with chillies. The heat level of a chilli is determined by the amount of capsaicin it contains. This compound is concentrated mainly in the ribs and seeds, so you can reduce the fieriness considerably by removing these parts. Chillies that have been pickled, or that are used raw, tend to have more heat than cooked chillies.

The heat level of a chilli is measured in Scoville units, on a scale where 0 is the heat level of a sweet pepper and 300,000 is the hottest chilli, the habañero. In many instances, the ratings have been simplified to a scale of 1–10, to make them easier to remember.

FRESH CHILLIES

The following are the most commonly used fresh chillies.

Jalapeño Heat level 6. One of the most common types of chilli, this is about the same length as a serrano, but plumper. Jalapeños are sold at all stages of ripeness, so you are as likely to find red as green. Green jalapeños are often pickled.

Serrano Heat level 8. This is a small chilli, about 4–5cm/1½–2in long and 1cm/½in wide, with a pointed tip. Serranos are used in cooked dishes, Guacamole and salsas.

Poblano *Heat level 3*. Like many chillies, poblanos are green, then ripen to a dark red. They are large, roughly 8cm/3½in long and 5.5cm/2¼in wide and are widely used in Mexican cooking. Anaheim chillies can be substituted for poblanos.

Fresno Heat level 8. Rather like long sweet peppers, fresnos are about 6cm/2½in long and 2cm/¾in wide. They have a hot, sweet flavour and are used in salsas, and meat, fish and vegetable dishes.

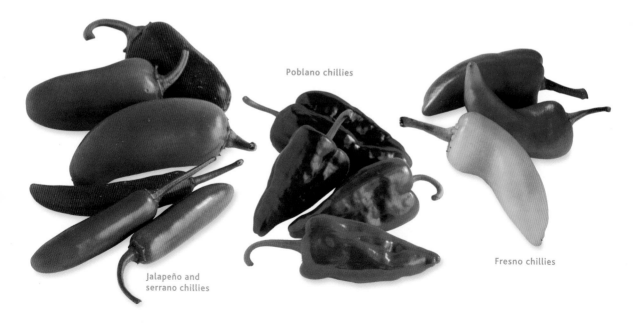

Poblano chillies

Fresno chillies

Jalapeño and serrano chillies

DRIED CHILLIES

Chillies were originally sundried, but today are more likely to be dried in an oven. In many cases, drying intensifies the flavour of chillies. Depending on the process used, drying can also impart extra flavour, as when jalapeños are dried and smoked. Not only does the flavour deepen to a rich smokiness, but the name of the chilli changes, and it becomes a chipotle.

The heat rating given for the dried chillies in the list that follows is based on the same scale as that used for the fresh chillies on the previous page. Dried chillies can be ground to a powder or cut into strips before being used. Unless the chillies are to be added to a dish with a high proportion of liquid, they are usually soaked in water before use.

The following is a list of some of the more common dried chillies, all of which feature in this book.

Ancho *Heat scale 3.* The most common dried chilli in Mexico, the ancho is a dried red poblano chilli, and has a fruity, slightly sharp flavour.

Cascabel *Heat scale 4.* The name means "little rattle" and refers to the noise that the seeds make inside the chilli. This chilli has a chocolate brown skin, and remains dark, even after soaking.

Chipotle *Heat scale 6.* These are smoked jalapeños. They add a wonderfully rich smoky flavour to all sorts of dishes, from barbecue sauces to chicken.

Guajillo *Heat scale 3.* Another popular dried chilli in Mexican cuisine, the guajillo is used in sauces or stews.

Habañero *Heat scale 10.* This is the grandaddy of them all, a chilli so hot that when it is puréed, even the fumes from the blender can scorch the skin. This chilli is also called Scotch Bonnet.

Pasada *Heat scale 3.* This chilli is crisply dried, and has citrus and apple flavours. It is used in soups and in sauces used for cooking meat or fish.

Pasilla *Heat scale 4.* Pasilla means "little raisin". This is the dried version of a fresh chilli called the chilaca. It is suitable for stuffing.

Chipotle chillies

Guajillo chillies

Ancho chillies

Cascabel chillies

Habañero chillies

Roasting and peeling chillies

1 Dry fry the chillies in a frying pan or griddle pan until the skins are scorched. Alternatively, spear them on a long-handled metal skewer and roast them over the flame of a gas burner until the skins blister and darken. Do not let the flesh burn.

2 Place the roasted chillies in a strong plastic bag and tie the top tightly to keep the steam in. Set aside for 20 minutes.

3 Remove the chillies from the bag and peel off the skins. Cut off the stalks, then slit the chillies and scrape out the seeds with a sharp knife. Wash your hands after handling the chillies.

Vegetables

Mexico's indigenous peoples were very good agriculturists, and when the Spanish invaded they found a country blessed with abundant vegetables, including corn, sweet potatoes, jicama, pumpkins and courgette (zucchini). The Spanish in turn introduced onions, garlic, runner (green) beans and cabbage, all of which were integrated into the Mexican cuisine.

CORN

The vegetable we know as corn, which flourishes in all the different climates and soils of Mexico, has been grown in the Americas for over five thousand years. It was brought to Europe by the Spanish in the late 15th century, but long before that it was a staple food of the indigenous peoples of Mexico, who used every part of the corn, including the husks and silks.

An ear of corn consists of yellow, plump kernels on a firm cob, sheathed in long green leaves or husks. Between the leaves and the kernels are long threads called silks, which are traditionally used for tying *tamales*.

Uses and cooking tips

Corn cobs can be cooked in boiling water, but do not add salt to the water or the kernels will toughen. Corn cobs can also be cooked in the oven or on the barbecue. In Mexico, corn is a popular street food. The husks are often used for wrapping food such as *tamales*, but they are not eaten.

To prepare corn, peel off the husks, then pull off the silks. (If necessary, scrub the cobs with a vegetable brush to remove any remaining silks.) If the corn is to be cooked on the barbecue, the husks can be pulled back, then replaced after removing the silks.

RUNNER BEANS

Runner (green) beans have been growing in the Americas for hundreds of years and are widely used, as are French or string beans. They should be bright and crisp, and are best eaten on the day they are bought if possible.

Uses and cooking tips

To prepare, top and tail the beans and remove any strings on the sides of the pods. Butter (lima) beans and broad (fava) beans must be removed from their soft, fleshy pods before use, and are sometimes blanched.

Mexicans use beans in salads and vegetable dishes. Beans are best cooked briefly in a pan of boiling water, or steamed until tender. These methods ensure the beans retain colour, texture and flavour and do not lose all their valuable nutrients.

BELOW: *Corn (left) is still encased in its husk; broad beans, runner beans, and French beans (right) are at their best when the pods are bright green and firm.*

LEFT: *Sweet potatoes can be baked or boiled and used in a salsa.*

ABOVE: *Jicama can be lightly boiled and eaten as a vegetable.*

SWEET POTATOES

One of the staple foods of the indigenous peoples of Mexico in pre-Columbian times, sweet potatoes are still a very important food. Sweet potatoes are starchy tubers, and need to be cooked before being eaten. There are many different varieties, ranging from pale-skinned sweet potatoes with pale crumbly flesh to darker tubers with thick skins and moist flesh. The skin colour of sweet potatoes can be from pink to deep purple, and the flesh can range from creamy white to the more familiar vivid orange.

Uses and cooking tips

Sweet potatoes are used in both sweet and savoury dishes, either cooked slowly in their skins or peeled and boiled. They are also used in stews and casseroles. They can be cooked in their skins (scrubbed first), or, if you prefer, peel them before boiling and mashing them.

RIGHT: Jicama *is delicious when it is used raw, such as in* jicama, *chilli and lime salad.*

JICAMAS

The *jicama* – or yam bean – is a native of Central America and spread to China. It looks like a turnip or beetroot, but has a conical base. The skin is light brown and quite thin. The moist, creamy-coloured flesh tastes slightly fruity. *Jicama* can be eaten raw or cooked. Look for firm *jicamas* that are about the size of a turnip.

Uses and cooking tips

Raw *jicama* makes a refreshing snack when it is sprinkled with freshly squeezed orange juice and served with chilli powder and salt. It is also delicious added to salads and used in salsas. *Jicama* retains its pleasingly crisp texture when boiled, as long as it is not overcooked. Mexicans like to use grated *jicama* in desserts.

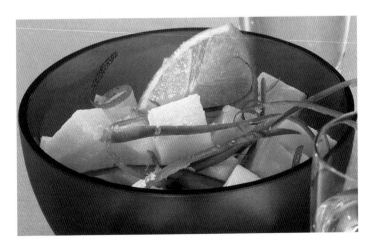

SQUASH

Pumpkins and other types of squash, cucumbers and *chayotes* all belong to the same family, and have been cultivated since ancient times. Pumpkin seeds dating back as far as 7000BC have been found in Mexico. The word "squash" comes from an Indian word, "askutasquash" meaning raw or uncooked, which may seem odd to those of us accustomed to eating squash cooked. However, there are numerous types of squash, and some are indeed delicious eaten raw.

There are two main classifications of squash – summer and winter. Many of the summer squash are now available all the year round, but it can still be useful to differentiate between the two distinct groups.

Summer squash grow on bushes and have thin, edible skins and soft seeds. Examples include courgette (zucchini), patty pans and vegetable marrows. The flesh is soft, generally pale in colour and has a high water content. It only needs a little cooking, and has a mild flavour. The seeds are dispersed through the flesh, and are usually eaten with it. Courgettes can be eaten raw, in salads.

Winter squash have harder, thicker skins and tough seeds. They may grow on bushes, but are often the fruit of vine plants. The skin is usually cut off and discarded, although if the squash is roasted, its skin may be soft enough to eat.

ABOVE: *Pumpkins are used in a variety of sweet and savoury dishes and are often roasted in large chunks with spices.*

Winter squash

Acorn, butternut, spaghetti, onion squash and pumpkin are some of the better known varieties. The flesh is often yellow or deep orange, is firmer and requires longer cooking than that of summer squash. When buying winter squash, choose specimens that are heavy for their size and that have unmarked skins. The seeds are generally removed and discarded before cooking, although some, such as pumpkin seeds, are a valuable food in their own right. The blossoms or flowers from both winter and summer squash are edible, and there are a number of Mexican recipes for cooking squash blossoms. In Mexico you can buy the blossoms separately, and they are sold in some speciality food shops elsewhere, but most cooks who want to try them will have to use home-grown vegetables. They are delicious coated in batter and fried.

BELOW: *Courgettes, marrow and patty pan squash are all summer squash.*

Uses and cooking tips

Summer squash can be steamed, stir-fried, boiled, baked or even coated in batter and deep fried. As the flesh is soft, it will only need to be cooked for a few minutes and should still retain some bite. Popular dishes are courgettes with cheese and chillies.

Winter squash are often cut into pieces, seeded and baked, steamed or boiled. They need to be cooked for longer than summer squash because the flesh is firmer. The skin is usually discarded, and this can be done either before cooking or after.

Mexicans often roast pumpkins in large chunks. They also cook pumpkin in water and sugar, as a dessert, or bake it with sugar and spices in the oven. Other types of squash are used in similar ways to pumpkins, and cooked squash often features as a filling in both sweet and savoury *empanadas* (pastries).

CHAYOTES

The *chayote* is native to Mexico. A member of the squash family, it grows on a vine, and goes under several names, including vegetable pear, *chocho* or *chow-chow*, *mirliton* and *choko*. *Chayotes* are pale green and pear-shaped, with smooth and leathery skins, which are often furrowed and may be covered with spines. Inside is a large, flat seed, which is edible. The flesh of the *chayote* is pale and crisp, like that of a tart green apple or a water chestnut.

Uses and cooking tips

Chayotes have a fairly mild flavour and are best peeled and served simply in salads or salsas, with a squeeze of lime or orange juice and some chillies. If they are cooked, they should be seasoned well. To cook *chayotes*, either peel and cook them in the same way as summer squash, or bake them.

BELOW: *Chayotes belong to the squash family, but they have a single, edible seed.*

Chorizo, dried meat and salt fish

In hot countries, dried and preserved foods are an important part of the diet. Mexico's traditional dried ingredients are very popular and are used to flavour many dishes.

CHORIZO

Chorizo is made from coarsely ground pork and spices. Chorizo first arrived with the Spanish conquistadors but has evolved into a distinctly Mexican sausage over the centuries. It is widely used in Mexican cookery in dishes such as eggs with chorizo (*huevos con chorizo*), soups, stews and casseroles.

BELOW: *Chorizo is a highly seasoned pork sausage that is frequently used to flavour various Mexican recipes.*

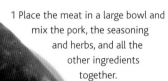

Mexican chorizo is made from fresh pork, unlike the Spanish chorizo, which is based upon smoked pork. The sausage mixture can be made up as needed and cooked immediately, just as it is, or packed into sausage skins. It can then be hung in a cool place and kept until required.

Making fresh chorizo

As is so often the case, bought sausages can be good, but there is little comparison to the homemade product. Chorizo is easy to make, and you can prepare it in bulk, then freeze the surplus. Air-drying is best left to the experts.

MAKES ABOUT 900G/2LB

900g/2lb pork mince
10ml/2 tsp each salt and ground
   black pepper
2.5ml/^{1}/$_2$ tsp freshly grated nutmeg
5ml/1 tsp dried thyme
2.5ml/^{1}/$_2$ tsp ground anise
2.5ml/^{1}/$_2$ tsp ground bay leaf
3 garlic cloves, crushed
120ml/4fl oz/^{1}/$_2$ cup sherry
   or brandy
juice of 2 limes

1 Place the meat in a large bowl and mix the pork, the seasoning and herbs, and all the other ingredients together.

2 Cover the bowl and chill in the refrigerator for at least 4 hours or preferably overnight, so that all the flavours fully blend together.

3 Fill sausage skins with the meat mixture to make individual sausages. Use the sausages immediately or freeze until required.

4 Cook by pricking the skins in several places with a fork or the point of a small sharp knife, then immersing the sausages in a large pan of boiling water. Continue to boil the sausages for at least 10 minutes or until the meat is thoroughly cooked.

5 If you prefer, you can shape the sausagemeat into small patties and fry these in a little fat, turning them once to ensure that they are cooked evenly on both sides.

6 Serve the sausages hot, with a spicy tomato-based sauce or chilli salsa, or abobo seasoning.

DRIED MEATS

Machaca is meat, usually beef, that has been salted and sun-dried before being shredded. This way of preparing meat is typical of northern Mexico, from Sonora in the west to Monterrey in the east.

Machaca is often mixed with scrambled eggs, beans and cheese and wrapped in a flour tortilla or with fried eggs for a hearty breakfast dish or served with beans and rice for dinner. *Machaca* is also often the meat in burritos, enchiladas and tacos. *Carne seca* (the term simply translates as "dried meat") is cut into chunks and served as an appetizer with fresh lime juice. It is one of the most popular dishes of the northern part of Mexico. *Machaca* is available in specialist delicatessens and Mexican grocery stores.

SALTED MEAT AND FISH

Salting was a useful way of preserving meat for long periods in the days before people had refrigerators and freezers. If a family slaughtered a pig or cow, every piece of the animal was utilized; by drying surplus meat or making it into sausages, it would have been possible to make it last for several months.

Fish was salted for much the same reason, but what began as a necessity is now a delicacy as Mexicans became very fond of fish prepared in this manner. Today, when the need for preserving fish is not as pressing, salt fish, particularly cod, is still popular in Mexican, Spanish, Caribbean and even French cooking. Available from many

ABOVE: *Salt cod, which has been salted and dried, has a very tough texture that requires long soaking before use.*

ethnic food stores and sometimes in supermarkets, salt cod is a useful ingredient because it can be kept in a cupboard for several months before use. The pieces on display look incredibly unappetizing and are rock hard. They are usually unwrapped and might have a slightly grimy appearance. Don't let this put you off: when it has been cleaned and rehydrated, salt fish is perfectly safe to cook with and consume.

Main uses and cooking tips

Before cooking, salt cod must be cleaned and soaked in a bowl of water for several hours, or overnight if possible. Changing the water often gets rid of any dirt or grit, reduces the salt content and softens the fish.

Making machaca at home

You will need 900g/2lb sirloin steak, about 5mm/1/2in thick and 45ml/3 tbsp medium ground sea salt to make this authentic dish.

Trim away any gristle from the meat and then sprinkle both sides with the sea salt. Make a hole in each piece of meat and thread string through, or hang the meat from a butcher's hook for about 3 days in a cool dry place so it can dry out. Alternatively, dry it out in an oven heated to the lowest setting.

When the meat is completely dry, place it in a bowl and pour over enough water to cover. Leave it to rehydrate for about 30 minutes. Drain the meat, and shred it finely with two forks. Spread it out to dry again. When it has dried, store it in a covered container in the refrigerator until required.

Cheese

Being a complete protein, cheese was an important addition to the Mexican diet. Until its arrival, Mexicans' main sources of protein were beans and corn, both of which are incomplete. Cheese is widely used in Mexican cooking. The type for each dish is carefully chosen, and the properties – crumbling, melting, grating – are as important as the flavour.

DEVELOPMENT OF CHEESE

In the history of Mexican cuisine, cheese arrived on the scene fairly late. Before the Conquest in 1521, the main source of meat was the pig, and there was therefore no milk. The Spanish invaders established vast estates and introduced dairy cattle to the country. Milk, cream and butter were produced, and the monks who travelled with the conquerors taught the local people how to make cheeses. At first these were based on traditional Spanish cheeses such as Manchego, but the Mexicans soon developed several cheeses of their own. Today, the range includes cheeses made from goat's and ewe's milk.

There are many different cheeses available in Mexico, but there are a few types that deserve special mention. Unfortunately, Mexican cheeses are seldom sold outside the country, so acceptable substitutes are suggested for cooks who are unable to access the authentic ingredient.

QUESO FRESCO

As the name suggests, *queso fresco* (fresh cheese) is young and unripened. *Queso fresco* is actually the generic name for a number of different cheeses, of all which share some common characteristics, being moist and creamy in colour, with a very mild flavour and a crumbly texture. The cheese is often used for crumbling over dishes such as scrambled eggs, cooked *nopales* (cactus leaves) or other vegetables. It is also used in tacos and other snacks based on tortillas and tostadas (Tostadas with shredded pork and spices). *Queso fresco* has a clean, sharp taste and is a good melting cheese. If you can't locate it, substitute a good quality ricotta or buffalo mozzarella, preferably bought from a specialist Italian delicatessen or food store.

Mozzarella

Ricotta

Queso anejo

Feta

ASADERO

The name means "roasting cheese" and this is a mild curd cheese that is beautifully supple. Asadero is best when it is melted, and is ideal for stuffing chillies or other vegetables or meats, as it is unlikely to leak out. The closest equivalent is mozzarella.

QUESO ANEJO

Anejo means "aged". This is a very mature, hard, dry cheese. Sharp and salty, it can be grated easily. Anejo is often used for sprinkling on the top of enchiladas. Parmesan cheese makes a good substitute.

BELOW: *Many Mexican cheeses are good for melting over the top of vegetable or meat dishes. Minguichi is a dip combining ancho or chipotle chillies, cheese and crema or crème fraîche.*

QUESO CHIHUAHUA

This is a soft white cow's-milk cheese available in braids, balls or rounds and resembles *anejo*, but is less salty. Substitute medium Cheddar cheese for it in recipes.

Monterey Jack

The Californian cheese called Monterey Jack originated as *queso del pais* ("country cheese"). Spanish missionaries taught the people of California to make it in the early part of the 18th century. The traditional recipe, which is still being used today, was refined in Monterey, California, about 200 years ago.

The "Jack" part of the name is reputed to owe its origin to David Jacks, who made the cheese in his

QUESO DE OAXACA

This is a stringy cheese that is ideal for cooking as it has good melting properties. It tastes slightly tart. Monterey Jack is recommended as a substitute in recipes.

dairy, the "s" being dropped when it was felt that the name Monterey Jack was more catchy. The cheese has a mild flavour and creamy texture and is good to eat on its own as well as being a useful cooking cheese. It matures well, developing a sweet, nutty flavour as it ages. Monterey Jack can be substituted in any recipe calling for *Queso de Oaxaca*, *asadero* or Chihuahua cheese. If you can't locate Monterey Jack, a mild Cheddar cheese can be used.

Herbs and spices

Mexican cooking makes use of a wide range of flavourings. Chillies are top of the list, but they are by no means the only flavourings used. Spices like cinnamon and allspice are popular and herbs also play a role. Some, such as **epazote**, *are native to the country, while others were introduced.*

ACHIOTE
This is the hard red-orange seed of the annatto tree, which is native to the warmer parts of South America, including some areas of Mexico. The seed is ground and added to food to give colour and flavour. Good quality, fresh achiote seeds give food a distinctive, earthy flavour. Achiote is used a lot in the Yucatán, where it is included in pastes that are spread on meats before cooking.

ALLSPICE
This tree is native to Jamaica, although it may also have grown naturally in the coastal area of Mexico around Tabasco. Columbus is reputed to have brought it to Europe from Jamaica, having mistaken the berries for peppercorns – the Spanish call the spice *pimienta*, which means pepper. Allspice berries are picked, dried and ground or used whole. They are used in various types of Escabeche to add flavour to vegetables or fish which is being pickled, and are also added to meat dishes. They even feature in desserts and drinks.

CINNAMON
Sri Lankan cinnamon is used quite extensively in Mexican cookery in both sweet and savoury dishes. It was introduced during the colonial era, and is a favourite spice in chorizo sausages. It is also used in rice pudding. It is sold in sticks whole or ready ground. Both ground cinnamon and cinnamon sticks are used in Mexican cooking, removing cinnamon sticks from the food before serving.

CLOVES
Brought to Mexico from Asia and Indonesia, via Spain, cloves were used for their aromatic and fiery flavour. Ground cloves are used in the complex spice mixes that are so important in making *moles* and *pepiáns*. Whole cloves can also be used when cooking with various types of meat and poultry.

Allspice

Cinnamon quills

Coriander leaf

Cumin

Ground cinnamon

Coriander seeds

Achiote

Cloves

CORIANDER

Fresh coriander leaves, called cilantro in Mexico, are used in a number of savoury dishes and salsas. The herb is native to Europe, but is grown in South America too. It has a wonderful flavour and aroma. Coriander seeds are also used in some Mexican recipes, but the two should not be confused, nor should one be substituted for the other, as they have very different flavours.

CUMIN SEEDS

Cumin seeds are ground with other spices in some savoury dishes, but are neither used alone nor in large quantities, as their taste would overpower other, more delicate flavours. Native to Egypt, cumin was introduced into Mexican cuisine during colonial times.

EPAZOTE

This herb is widely used in Mexican cooking, but is, unfortunately, not available outside Mexico unless you grow it yourself. There is no real substitute for the distinctive, sharply pungent flavour of this fresh herb. *Epazote* is also useful because when it is cooked with beans such as black beans, it can help to relieve flatulence.

OREGANO

Several varieties of oregano are grown in Mexico. The most popular type is from the verbena family; its flavour is stronger and more aromatic than that of the European varieties. Sold fresh or dried in markets across Mexico, oregano adds a delightful sweet note to Escabeche, stews and meat dishes.

TAMARIND

The dark brown, bean-shaped pod comes from the tamarind tree, which has grown in India for centuries. The Spanish introduced it to the West Indies in the 17th century. Tamarind is usually sold as a pressed block of pods and pulp – rather like a block of pressed stoned dates – and is often sold in Indian food shops. The taste is a refreshing mixture of sweet and sour.

VANILLA

Records depicting Aztec life reveal that they were familiar with vanilla, and there is also evidence that it was used in Mexico in the 16th century as a flavouring for hot chocolate. Vanilla pods grow on vines, and until the 1800s, the spice was grown exclusively in Mexico. Good quality pods are very dark brown, waxy and malleable. The spice has a rich aroma and a sweet taste. It is perfect for adding to desserts and is also used to flavour drinks. Vanilla sugar is great in cakes, puddings and other sweet dishes, and one pod will flavour several jars full of sugar before it is exhausted.

Vanilla sugar

Vanilla pods

Oregano

Tamarind

Alcoholic drinks

Mexico has a large number of fermented beverages, mainly derived from fruit or a plant called the agave. Many of these are acquired tastes and not particularly popular outside the country.

BEER

Mexicans were introduced to the brewing process by the German settlers who came to their country and many of the brewing companies in existence today have German roots. Mexican beer production centres largely around the north of the country. The city of Monterrey in Nuevo León is renowned as the beer capital of Mexico. Mexican beer brands such as Dos Equis, Sol and Corona are exported, although these are often brewed outside Mexico on licence. Other brands, such as Tecate, which are less readily available, are worth trying.

WINE

Wine production on a large scale was actively discouraged during the years of Spanish rule as the conquerors wanted to promote wines and spirits from Spain. A wine industry finally did grow up, however, in Baja California, and even today, the major vineyards are in the north-west of the country, although there is some wine production further south. The popular grapes for the production of white wine are Chardonnay, Sauvignon Blanc, Riesling and Chenin Blanc, while established red grape varieties include Cabernet Sauvignon, Pinot Noir, Grenache and Merlot.

ABOVE: *Pulque is a Mexican alcoholic drink that is prepared from the fermented sap of agave plants.*

PULQUE

Records from the time of Cortés make reference to *pulque* being drunk by the Aztecs. It is a beer-like drink made from the sap of the agave plant, which is commonly called *maguey* in Mexico. While chocolate drinks were the preserve of the ruling classes in 16th century Mexico, *pulque* was drunk by the common people. The drink is still very popular, and small bars selling *pulque* are widespread. These bars were reputed to be wild, dangerous and inhospitable places.

KAHLÚA

This is a coffee liqueur made in Mexico city and popular worldwide. It is added to fresh coffee to make after-dinner coffee and often features in cocktails. Kahlúa is delicious when drunk from a straight liqueur glass with a thin layer of cream floated on the top, and it can also be blended with a scoop or two of vanilla ice cream.

MESCAL

This is the generic name for Mexican distilled spirit made from the agave plant. Tequila is just one type of *mescal*. In western Europe, the name *mescal* is synonymous with one brand of the spirit, which has a *maguey* worm in the bottle. This has led to drinking sessions to see who lands with the worm, and the reputation of *mescal* suffered in the process.

BELOW: *Kahlua is a coffee liqueur that is delicious as a drink and as a dessert when mixed with ice cream.*

TEQUILA

Without doubt, tequila is the Mexican spirit which is best known outside the country. A specific type of *mescal*, it is made from the distilled sap of the blue agave plant native to Mexico.

The Spanish taught Mexicans the art of distilling. *Pulque*, the national drink made from the agave plant, was the perfect subject, and they began by distilling it to make *mescal*. This was then distilled a second time to produce tequila.

Tequila takes its name from the eponymous town in Jalisco where it was first made. The name means "volcano" in the local Indian dialect. Jalisco is also the home of *mariachi* music, which may explain how tequila gained its image as a fun, party drink.

There are two general categories of tequila: tequila 100 per cent agave (premium tequila which must be bottled at source) and tequila, made of at least 51 per cent agave (the rest is usually maize or sugarcane). There are four types of tequila: blanco (white, standard tequila), oro (gold, mellowed by colours and flavourings), reposado (blanco kept for up to a year) and anejo (blanco aged for more than a year).

Tequila drinking

Drinking a shot of tequila in the classic manner, with a lick of salt beforehand and a wedge of lime after, is one of the best ways for Europeans to sample this drink. The method was originally adopted because the spirit was so crude that salt and lime were deemed necessary to make it palatable.

A natural progression from the shot was the margarita. The rim of the glass is dipped in salt, the lime juice and tequila are combined and triple sec (orange liqueur) is added. A margarita may be served neat, over ice, or with crushed ice. In Mexico, tequila is sipped alternately with *sangrita*, tomato juice flavoured with chillies and seasonings. When tequila and tomato juice are combined, the drink becomes a Bloody Maria.

Mescal

Tequila

Tequila blanco

Tequila and lime

Margarita

Index